Technology Transfer to Cities

Other Titles in This Series

Also of Interest

Westview Special Studies in Science, Technology, and Public Policy

Technology Transfer to Cities:
Processes of Choice at the Local Level
W. Henry Lambright

This study breaks new ground in concentrating on *who* innovates and *how* innovation occurs in the city. It is based on twenty case histories constructed during a two-year study of technological change in the public sectors of metropolitan Syracuse and Rochester, New York. The cases reflect most functions of urban government and cover a wide range of hardware and managerial technology. They shed light on little-known areas of technology and urban life.

The study draws conclusions about the stimuli that cause local bureaucrats to seek technological solutions to problems; the ways in which bureaucrats overcome opposition to the adoption of new technologies; and the allocation of resources necessary to effect the solutions. The marketing abilities and strategies necessary to obtain local decisions in favor of new technologies are emphasized, as is the importance of an effective implementation coalition once a technology is "bought."

Ultimately, what is wanted is routine use—incorporation. Once the technological innovation has become part of the system, the need for the entrepreneurial role disappears.

W. Henry Lambright is professor of political science and public administration at the Maxwell School, Syracuse University, and director of the Science and Technology Policy Center at the Syracuse Research Corporation.

Technology Transfer to Cities: Processes of Choice at the Local Level

W. Henry Lambright

with the assistance of Paul J. Flynn, Albert H. Teich, and Alfreda B. Lakins

Westview Press / Boulder, Colorado

54285

Westview Special Studies
in Science, Technology, and Public Policy

This report was prepared with the support of National Science Foundation's contract number RDA-75-19704. Any options, findings, conclusions, or recommendations expressed in this document are those of the authors and do not necessarily reflect the views of NSF.

Copyright © 1979 by Westview Press, Inc.

Published in 1979 in the United States of America by
Westview Press, Inc.
5500 Central Avenue
Boulder, Colorado 80301
Frederick A. Praeger, Publisher

Library of Congress Cataloging in Publication Data
Lambright, W. Henry, 1939-
    Technology transfer to cities.
    (Westview special studies in public policy and public systems management)
    Includes index.
    1. Municipal government—United States. 2. Municipal services—United States.
3. Technological innovations—United States. 4. Technology transfer. I. Title.
JS331.L35   352'.008'0973   78-23863
ISBN 0-89158-366-1

Printed and bound in the United States of America

Contents

Tables

*Dedicated to
Dan and Nat,
two boys who
love cities*

Preface

In March 1974, Albert Teich and I completed a report, *Federal Laboratories and Technology Transfer: Institutions, Linkages, and Processes*, based on a research project for the National Science Foundation. This report addressed the factors that facilitated and impeded the transfer of new technology (hardware and managerial) to various users. Those users were to be found in industry and federal, state, and local governments. We discovered that a multi-institutional (interorganizational) approach to the transfer of a technology could help to accelerate its utilization. If the federal agencies and their laboratories, the manufacturers (suppliers), and various public and private users would work in partnership early in the process, technology would be transferred. Otherwise, failures of communication, misunderstandings, and disagreements would create barriers to full utilization.

The laboratory transfer study had been initiated from the federal perspective. It began with a focus on the producer of the technology. Obviously, full understanding of the transfer process required better comprehension of the role of other organizations, especially that of users. This was particularly the case where the users were local governments and the technologies related to specific public service sectors such as urban mass transportation, education, fire protection, and housing.

What were the dynamics of the local innovation process? Why did cities adopt or reject certain technologies? Why did they implement some adopted technologies while permitting others to lie fallow, terminate, or be so transformed as to be unrecognizable as those initially acquired? At what point could it be said that full use occurred? Adoption and implementation did not necessarily mean incorporation or institutionalization of an innovation.

These questions were of immediate public policy relevance. Support was gained from the National Science Foundation for a broad study of the adoption and use of urban technology. I wrote the proposal in spring 1975 with the assistance of Paul Flynn, then a graduate student at Maxwell School, Syracuse University. The study was funded by the National Science Foundation in September 1975 and became a major research effort to which my associates and I devoted ourselves for the next two years. We used a decision-making approach that aimed at delineating the relations between forces helping and hindering innovation in local public services. This book is based on the report derived from that project, *Adoption and Utilization of Urban Technology: A Decision-Making Study*. To produce that report, we prepared twenty case histories of specific experiences in the attempted introduction of urban technologies that were new to the adopters in question.

A number of very able individuals participated in the project. First, there was Paul Flynn who served as project manager, wrote eight of the twenty case histories, and contributed greatly to the analysis in the final report. Second, there was Albert Teich who provided astute guidance both to case writers and to me and who wrote most of chapter 4 of this volume. Third, there was Alfreda Lakins, a remarkable combination of secretary, editor, and writer, who summarized the twenty cases for the analysis in the form seen in chapter 3. In addition to the above, the following people also deserve recognition for their research, writing, or supervision of the work of others in connection with the case histories: Marguerite Beardsley, James Carroll, John DeMarco, Thomas Dorsey, Daisy Goldstein, Patrick Hennigan, Barbara Howard, Richard Kozel, Deborah Roberts, and Robert Roberts. Finally, a special word of thanks is owed David Roessner, of the National Science Foundation, who monitored the project. He helped in ways that only those of us on the project could really appreciate. To be sure, neither he nor the National Science Foundation should be held responsible for the interpretations presented here.

Ultimately, of course, every project has a principal investigator who pulls it all together and tries to present the work of many in a way that reads as though it came from the pen of a single individual. I was "P.I." on the project and I am principal author of this book. As one who previously had played the author role via the lone-scholar approach, this task of being author-orchestrator was new and refreshing. It also had its frustrations and problems. Whatever else, it kept me very, very busy. Through it all, my wife, Nancy, was a source of help and encouragement. My sons, Dan and Nat, bore up well under the burden of a preoccupied father. I hope that the project, the report, and this book will add a bit to our understanding of an increasingly important subject: the application of new technology to urban problems. If so, all the effort will have proved worthwhile.

W.H.L.

1
Introduction

The Problem

In recent years, the problem of technology transfer to domestic social needs has become one of the more controversial and nettlesome issues in the relations between the federal government and cities. As funding for federal research and development has increased for domestic-oriented agencies such as the Departments of Housing and Urban Development, Transportation, Justice, and Energy, it has become painfully clear that spending money for research and development does not guarantee innovation.

Innovation is a broader concept that involves the utilization of new technology. Federal agencies may help to create technology, but they are not the users of such technology. The users are, for the most part, state and local governments, private industry, and ultimately the general public. The consequence is a separation, a gap between the institutions and processes of technology creation and those concerned with its utilization. Bridging that gap requires technology transfer—a conscious effort on the part of federal agencies to move technology from research and development to implementation.

Our concern is with the specific issues related to technology transfer to the city (i.e., urban public services). This is a subset of the broader problem of technology transfer, but it is an extremely significant part of the whole.[1] Urban services touch the individual in virtually every way, from the education of children to protection from criminals to the disposal of garbage. How those services are managed impacts on the most fundamental aspects of quality of life. To the extent that local public services might be improved through better hardware and managerial techniques, they would appear an apt focus for federal technology transfer efforts. On occasion, they have been. However, most students of technology transfer are persuaded that federal efforts to date have been less than successful in accomplishing their goals. Many hardware and managerial innovations that could be helpful in mitigating urban problems are lying fallow. Either they are not adopted by their intended users, or, if adopted, they are not implemented and placed into routine service. They are often abandoned or so diluted that they cease to be innovative in any sense.

There are some who say that the reason is simply that there is not enough technology-push from the federal government or innovative companies. According to this point of view, demonstration projects and more aggressive public information techniques (i.e., marketing) would sell the technology. Others say that there is already plenty of technology-push. As they see it, the problem is the lack of demand-pull from cities. This perspective finds local government inherently uninnovative. It regards municipal officials as unwilling or unable to take the necessary risks entailed in utilizing new technology.

The argument that local government is uninnovative has an attractive ring. The position that urban bureaucracies are at fault coincides with conventional wisdom, general attitudes, and even some economic theory.[2] Plenty of examples of laggard local government can be found. In his article "Fighting Fires: Only the Truck Is New," Alan Frohman reports that most fire departments across the United States continue to fight fires with nineteenth-century technology and techniques. He notes:

> Water remains the principal extinguishing agent; the fire department's job is to deliver the pumps, hoses, nozzles, and men needed to get the water onto the fire. Delivery by truck, powered by an internal combustion engine, has replaced delivery by horse-drawn wagon; that is the only obvious change.[3]

Frohman goes on to lament the continued use of "archaic

and outmoded" technology by local public-service agencies, for what is true for firefighting is also found to be the situation for law enforcement, sanitation, education, and other local departmental services.

"If we can go to the moon, why can't we innovate in cities?" That question is asked over and over again. The answers vary depending upon who is responding.[4] One response that is frequently stated, although seldom put on paper, is that the men and women who govern urban America are either technically backward or incapable of taking risks.

One can accept the position that there is need for more demand-pull from local government, however, without agreeing with the analysis of why such a demand is weak. Local public officials may be rejecting new hardware not because they are uninnovative but because they are behaving rationally in light of their view of the problems and the range of solutions that are available to them.

Local government officials are not in the business of inventing or supplying technology. Their business is delivering public services and solving local problems. In performing these tasks, they make decisions, some of which involve the adoption and use of hardware and managerial techniques that are innovative (i.e., new, from the standpoint of those adopting them).

An innovative technology is not an end in itself; it is a means, a tool. The degree to which an innovative tool is diffused depends on a multitude of factors of immense complexity. George Downs and Lawrence Mohr have stressed this in pointing to the instability of findings in empirical studies of innovation. They state, "Factors found to be important for innovation in one study are found to be considerably less important, or not important at all, or even important in the reverse direction in another study."[5]

Downs and Mohr were speaking as scholars dealing with the innovation literature in general. However ill-understood innovation may be, the subject of innovation in local public services is even less charted. In view of this complexity, a degree of caution, humility, and a realization that there are no simple answers are essential in approaching the subject of technology transfer to the city. Even where the federal government and private sector are pushing and local officials want to innovate, there may be other factors operating to minimize the actual transfer process.

What are these factors? What are the key variables that affect what happens or does not happen where new technology meets the city? This study was undertaken because there is so much rhetoric about the subject of technology transfer to the city and so little concrete knowledge about it. The aim of the study is exploratory. Its approach is the reverse of the usual where technology transfer is concerned. We are turning technology transfer on its head, so to speak, looking at the processes of technological choice from a user's, rather than a producer's, perspective. This approach will indicate why and how cities innovate and the role that federally initiated transfer processes play (or fail to play) in local decision-making processes.

It is absolutely clear that the process of technological innovation at the local level is far more complicated than conventional wisdom, academic theory, or federal policy would tend to suggest. Understanding this subject may well begin with an appreciation of what it takes and who it takes to innovate at the local level.

The Approach

In order to probe the factors that cause the demand, or lack thereof, for new technology at the local level, it is necessary to understand the relationship between innovation and urban decision making. While a great deal has been written about both, little has been written about them in relation to one another. The innovation and urban decision-making literatures are distinct from one another. Students of innovation have seldom studied cities. Urban scholars have not generally been interested in innovations in the delivery of public services. To understand urban innovation, however, the two intellectual traditions must be synthesized.

Innovation and Decision-Making Traditions

Most theories of innovation begin with the classical

diffusion model. As stated by Everett Rogers, this model holds that "an innovation is communicated via certain channels to members of a social system who adopt it over a period of time."[6] Most studies of innovation examine specific members of a social system, such as farmers and their adoption of hybrid seeds. Studies also tend to focus on a specific decision to adopt at a particular point in time. As a consequence, innovation research tends not to study decisions by collective bodies, nor does it give "time" its due. The fact that decision making is a process rather than a single act is often ignored.[7]

The lack of congruence between this tradition and the reality of urban innovation can be seen in the fact that most important changes in the city are the consequence of collective acts, sometimes even involving votes of the people, as in fluoridation decisions.[8] Moreover, the factor of time matters. The collective entity that decides to adopt the innovation may well be replaced by another collective entity that implements it. Over time, decision makers change, and the technology is affected by these changes. Adoption means little if the technology is not implemented.

Urban scholars have only recently been interested in the problems of urban service delivery.[9] For years, much brainpower was devoted to determining the degree to which local power elites did or did not govern cities. Such elites may once have been important in larger cities. They may still be key in certain small cities. However, the consensus among urban scholars, at least those with a political science orientation, is that leadership in local government depends upon the issue.[10] Rather than suffering from concentrated power, cities are increasingly plagued by too much fragmentation in authority.[11] In some respects, we have gone from the view that few govern to the view that no one is in charge.[12] In neither case do we know much about the relation of urban government to innovation in local services.

A Process Model for Urban Innovation

An approach is needed which recognizes that innovation in cities is collective and occurs over time. It must be one that sees innovation as involving the processes of government and, hence, the uses of political power. Such an approach requires going beyond existing innovation and urban decision-making literatures. It necessitates a model that is dynamic regarding time as well as relationships among actors in a local setting. In our view, a useful framework is a process model that combines an understanding of the stages of innovation with an action-forcing unit of analysis. The one describes what happens; the other shows who makes it happen. Answers to how and why emerge from applying this model to case studies of urban innovation.[13]

Stages of Innovation

The notion of innovation as a process occurring over time is essential. At least four decision stages are subsumed under the term innovation. These are preadoption, adoption, implementation, and incorporation.

1. *Preadoption.* Preadoption is the period that extends from the time someone in local government becomes aware of a problem or opportunity requiring some kind of response, to the time an innovation is placed on an official agenda for local adoption. Thus, it encompasses awareness and agenda-setting substages.

2. *Adoption.* In the local government context, adoption can be operationalized as a decision to allocate scarce local resources to a particular new technology. Such resources generally are financial. However, in certain cases, they may be in a different form, for example, the authority to grant a license to permit a private sector entity to provide a new urban service. If the resource is financial, it is not necessary that the total financial burden be assumed locally. However, there must be evidence of some local commitment shown through the allocation of funds over which the local adopter has control, as in matching funds for a federally sponsored program.

In a sense, adoption is the beginning of one decision-making process and the culmination of another. Adoption is the gradual matching of a local government need with an innovative technology in the political context of a city. The innovation may have been placed on a decision maker's agenda, but its adoption represents a decision to allocate money. Such a decision may require a search that yields solutions other than the innovative one. Perhaps small-scale pilot tests take place and are evaluated. Possibly consultants are hired. Much depends upon the scale of the technology involved as well as the nature of the problem. From this procedure may emerge the formal adoption of a particular innovative solution or, just as easily, a rejection of the innovation in question in favor of some other solution.

This view of adoption thus reveals it as part of a larger process of many smaller decisions leading to it. This model indicates that decision making is sequential. It places local choices in a problem-solving mode. Problems and solutions gradually are better defined and linked over time.[14]

3. *Implementation.* The third major decision stage in the innovation process occurs when the local government tests the chosen solution in an operating environment. As used here, the term implementation refers to trial usage as distinguished from incorporation, the next decision stage. A policy is implemented to introduce new technology. But policies can be changed, rejected, or avoided at the implementation stage.[15] During implementation, use of the technology is expanded with further testing, training of practitioners, and a gradual meshing of technology with what is acceptable in a real-world environment. It is quite conceivable that the technology may be abandoned at this stage on the basis of better governmental knowledge as to what the technology can and cannot do. Or it may be dropped because others, perhaps external to the city, who contribute to its support withdraw their subsidy. However, if local reactions to the technology are favorable, local commitment may be so great that it will become needed rather than merely desired. And what is needed will be supported by local sources, irrespective of funding policies external to the city.

4. *Incorporation.* Technologies that become needed are incorporated.[16] They become part of the routines of local government services. Exactly when a technology becomes incorporated is not easy to say. In some instances, local money must replace federal demonstration money, and this may

provide the clearest indication that the decision to incorporate has been made. However, incorporation implies more than financial support. It conveys a notion that a technology is no longer on trial but has been accepted. It is routine, no longer new. Rejection or termination is not an option being seriously entertained. The bias in local decision making has shifted from a "push to begin" to a "pull to retain" an essential public service tool.

Participants and Relationships

The local innovation process has more than a temporal aspect, of course. It entails relationships among participants in that process. The nature of those relationships, not some inherent dynamic of "autonomous technology,"[17] moves an innovation forward from preadoption to incorporation. However, such relationships can also prevent forward motion.

The fundamental relationship is between a collective decision maker called "the city" and a technology. The city is perceived as a user. Who decides on behalf of the user? The answer is local government. However, local government is also a collectivity consisting of such actors as legislators, mayors, and bureaucrats. In local government, who decides or moves others to decide? Obviously, the problem of relationships is more complex than it appears to be in recent work that emphasizes an "organization-innovation" dyad.[18] Such a model is more applicable to private sector than public sector innovation.

Public organizations such as local agencies decide in a political environment, consisting of other institutions that help determine how they relate to the innovation. Moreover, it is much easier to note the roles that must be aggregated to obtain a complete innovation (an innovation that has gone through all four stages) than to explain how this is accomplished. Suffice it to say here that adoption and use of urban technology is a collective decision-making process. Certain roles must be linked into a support system for an innovation. This is essential to overcome whatever barriers may stand in its path. Under optimum conditions, the following roles would appear to be essential to a complete coalition: adopters, implementers, clients, and suppliers. The first three represent the city in its role of technology user. The supplier is the institution in the background. All roles must be brought together if an urban innovation process is to reach culmination. These roles are delineated in the following paragraphs.

1. *Adopters.* Adopters are those who have official and formal authority to make decisions to allocate local resources to new technology. Usually, these include the top management of the line agency, the budget office, the mayor or manager, and the city council (and possibly others, depending upon the form of local government).

2. *Implementers.* We distinguish between those who make policy decisions (adopters) and those who actually implement policy (implementers). In theory, this is a distinction between policy and administration, between politicians and bureaucrats. In reality, this distinction is not so clear. Top administrators bridge the gap from policy formation to policy implementation. However, middle managers and employees are more in the realm of pure implementers.

3. *Clients.* In general, local government is accountable to the public. In addition, specific agencies are informally accountable to a particular clientele, those who receive services from the agencies. The role of the general public and this clientele may vary among innovations and functions of local government, partly because of the proximity of organizational users and the people they serve.

4. *Suppliers.* Local governments (adopters, implementers) are users of technology. They do not manufacture technology. Hence, there must be a manufacturer and/or distributor to supply technology, at least where hardware innovations are concerned. Managerial techniques are generally provided to cities by consulting firms and sometimes by professional associations.

To achieve a complete innovation in local public services, these four roles must coalesce around the innovation sooner or later. Adopters, implementers, and clients must want it, and there must be a supplier able and willing to provide the innovation at a price the city is willing to pay. Such mobilization of support does not occur automatically. A fifth role is needed. This is the role of entrepreneur, a catalyst creating a "minimum winning coalition"[19] of members representing the other four roles.

5. *Entrepreneurs.* Entrepreneurs put action into process. They contribute the local push behind decision making. The role of entrepreneur can be filled by various individuals and organizations; entrepreneurs can be adopters, implementers, clients, or suppliers. As entrepreneurs, however, they play the special additional role of forming links among the other local actors. Where necessary, they create alliances between local government and external organizations. In doing so, they form a coalition sufficient to move the innovation from one stage to another.

Entrepreneurs become the action-forcing element in the local innovation process. Coalitions that involve some or all of the other local roles must be formed to achieve adoption, implementation, and incorporation. What it takes for a coalition at one stage may be different at another stage. Yet, incorporation requires explicit or implicit commitments from all four sets of participants. Indeed, one mark of incorporation may be the disappearance of the entrepreneurial role. With incorporation, there is no further need for an entrepreneurial function.

Our model permits the study of innovation as a dimension of urban decision making. It does not say whether a particular innovation is good or bad; rather, it indicates whether it is successful or unsuccessful in terms of being complete or incomplete. It demonstrates what happens and who makes it happen at the local level. Given an appropriate data base, this approach reveals why and how innovation processes take the paths they do, and why some innovations transfer while others do not.

The Choice of Cities

The problem addressed is technology transfer to the city. The approach is a process model emphasizing local entrepreneurship and coalition building. The data base is drawn from twenty decision-making case histories of specific innovations. The decisions cut across various urban service areas and are drawn from recent experience in two cities: Syracuse and Rochester, New York.

The choice of cities was governed by both methodological and practical considerations. Our aim was to study decision making by local government. We were interested in local government, rather than particular innovation. This meant that instead of studying one innovation that diffused to many settings, we examined, in depth, two settings exposed to a variety of innovations. We wished to understand particular innovative processes in a cross section of local public services. We wanted comparison among service areas, as well as between cities. Given the realities of time and money, two cities were deemed sufficient for the exploratory analysis contemplated. We needed to immerse ourselves in these two locales.

Syracuse and Rochester were chosen because they were reasonably typical of middle-sized cities in the United States. Syracuse, in particular, is used by industry for market testing of new products because it is regarded to be representative of northeastern urban America. Rochester is less representative, but it allows a comparison with Syracuse that is extremely interesting from the standpoint of this study. Rochester is widely regarded as an innovative city. It has an image of being perhaps the most progressive city in the state. If innovations should succeed anywhere, we expected they would in the favorable climate of Rochester.

In addition to these reasons, Syracuse and Rochester were chosen because the nature of the study demanded close attention to detail. We reside in Syracuse and can easily drive the 90 miles to Rochester. Proximity permits us the opportunity to observe decision-making events in progress. This is an invaluable asset, given the difficulties of knowing who is doing what and how from a distance. In our view, the Syracuse-Rochester experience in urban technology is important in its own right. It is even more significant for what it tells us about innovation in cities generally. We do not suggest this study is the final word on urban technology and its governance. We do regard it as a necessary beginning.

2
The Setting:
Syracuse and Rochester

The local settings for the technologies studied are the Syracuse and Rochester metropolitan areas. It might once have been possible to study urban technology in a context that was wholly contained within the political boundaries of the cities of Syracuse and Rochester, but this is no longer true. What is apparent from the perspective of one viewing these two cities from an airplane is increasingly obvious to those who live there—urbanization is rapidly transfiguring the face of the cities and all of the surrounding communities. In 1961, Martin et al. wrote *Decisions in Syracuse*,[20] a collection of decision-making cases aimed at revealing the existence or nonexistence of a local power elite. In undermining the power elite thesis, they pointed out the diffusion of decision-making centers in Syracuse. They found that it was no longer possible to speak of Syracuse without reference to the larger metropolitan entity of which it had become an inextricable part. The same could just as easily have been said of Rochester. The logic of this approach has become more compelling with each passing year. We speak of Syracuse and Rochester, but we increasingly find Onondaga and Monroe Counties constituting the setting that approximates the reality of many urban public services.

Population, People, and Wealth

As population sprawled into neighboring towns and villages, the rustic character of Onondaga and Monroe Counties changed. In many ways, with the exception of political jurisdiction, Greater Syracuse and Greater Rochester have become coterminous with their counties. Reality is forcing administrators at every jurisdictional level to recognize the need for changes in the way local services are delivered. The needs of the cities have outraced the capacity of city government to provide for them, and both Onondaga and Monroe Counties have begun, often reluctantly, to assume more and more tasks that were previously performed by city government. However, these jurisdictional changes are coming slowly.

The setting of urban technology in the two "greater" cities is thus one of changing city-county relations. The center-cities face the problems of decline, while the urbanizing outlying towns cope with those of growth. Both the city and noncity residents want services; the types of services they want may differ, however, as do their abilities to pay for what they desire.

In short, Greater Syracuse and Greater Rochester may be seen as rather typical urban settings where public services are concerned. They may also be seen as having relationships with technology that are similar to those other cities have had. In many ways, the cities have been shaped by manufacturing, transportation, and other technologies over which little control has been exerted. Both are now more consciously seeking to use technology to solve their problems and shape their destinies.

Both Syracuse and Rochester are declining in population while the populations of the counties in which they are located are on the rise. The U.S. Bureau of the Census cites that in 1960 the population of the city of Syracuse was 216,038 and that of Onondaga County was 423,028. By 1970, the city had a population of only 197,297, and the county had grown to 472,835. Similarly, the population of Rochester in 1960 was 318,611, and that of Monroe County was 586,387. By 1970, Rochester declined to 295,011, and Monroe County spurted to 711, 917 (see Table 1).

Not only are the populations of the cities declining, but they also are changing in composition. Successive waves of immigration have given Syracuse and Rochester a mixture of ethnic groups: Irish, Italian, German, etc. (In Syracuse,

Table 1

POPULATION AND PER CAPITA INCOME

	New York State	Monroe County	Rochester	Onondaga County	Syracuse
1960 Pop.	16,782,304	586,387	318,611	423,028	216,038
1970 Pop.	18,241,391	711,917	295,011	472,835	197,297
1975 Pop.	18,075,487	708,642	267,172	472,708	182,543
% Change 1960-1975	+7.7	+20.9	-16.1	+11.7	-15.5
1960 Income	2236	2295	2068	2132	2152
1970 Income	3608	3821	3238	3386	3158
1975 Income	4903	5311	4335	4691	4123
% Change 1960-1975	119.3	131.4	109.6	120.0	91.6

Sources: U. S. Bureau of the Census. County and City Data Book, 1972; and Population Estimates and Projections series, P-25, No. 680, May 1977.

particularly, the ethnic variation bears a striking similarity to overall ethnic differences in the Northeast, one factor that makes Syracuse a favorite city for market surveys.) In both Syracuse and Rochester, the early immigrant groups tended to settle in their own sections of the city, forming ethnic communities within the city. However, as the second and third generations became Americanized, some moved to new neighborhoods, particularly in the surrounding suburbs. Most recently, the waves of migrants have been poor nonwhite minorities. In 1950, about 2 percent of the populations of Syracuse and Rochester were nonwhite (Table 2). By 1970, the figures stood at 12 percent nonwhite in Syracuse and 17.6 percent in Rochester.

As the population has changed racially, it has also changed in age. Senior citizens have tended to remain in the city, keeping their homes or apartments in established neighborhoods or moving into new high-rise apartments built especially for them. Each of the cities has 4 percent more people over 65 years of age than their counties (Table 3). In short, both

Table 2

NON-WHITE POPULATION
(Percent of Total Population)

	1950 Total (Percent)	1960 Total (Percent)	1970 Total (Percent)
Monroe Co.	8247 (1.7)	25,067 (4.3)	56,096 (7.9)
Rochester	7845 (2.4)	24,228 (7.6)	52,115 (17.6)
Onondaga Co.	6275 (1.8)	14,094 (3.3)	26,776 (5.7)
Syracuse	5058 (2.3)	12,281 (5.7)	23,597 (12.0)

Source: New York State Division of the Budget. New York State
Statistical Yearbook, 1974.

Syracuse and Rochester are gaining people who require
services, but these cities are not as able to support them as in the
past.

These changes in population in the city and county are
reflected in relative wealth. Monroe County is a wealthy county
(Table 1). Some of the Rochester suburbs, especially Brighton
and Pittsford, are among the wealthiest in the nation. Per
capita income in Monroe County by 1975 was $400 greater than
that of New York State, which is a relatively wealthy state. In
contrast, per capita income in Onondaga County was $200 less
than the state level but was closing the gap. The cities have less
per capita income than the counties, and the income difference
is widening (Table 4). In 1960, per capita income in Syracuse
was greater than that in Onondaga County. By 1975, per capita
income in Syracuse was 88 percent that of the county. The
situation in Rochester is equally striking. The income
differential between Rochester and Monroe County is 18
percent. The statistics thus reflect the syndrome of urban
decline.

Similarly, Table 5 presents per capita data on taxation, debt,
and expenditures for the two areas in 1965 and 1974. Items one
through four show that the two cities are less well-off,
financially, than are the counties. The cities are using almost
all their property taxation authority. The Rochester area is

Table 3

POPULATION AGED OVER 65 YEARS
(Percent of Population)

	1950	1960	1970
New York State	8.5	10.1	10.8
Monroe Co.	10.0	10.8	9.7
Rochester	11.0	14.0	13.7
Onondaga Co.	9.1	9.5	9.3
Syracuse	9.5	12.1	13.0

Source: U.S. Bureau of the Census.   County and City Data Book,
          1972, 1967, 1957.

also more heavily taxed than is the Syracuse area. The city of Rochester has been especially hard hit with increased property taxes in the past decade.

Per capita debt has dramatically increased since 1965 in both areas. Both counties have outpaced the upstate average, with Onondaga County having overtaken Monroe County. The biggest problem is in Rochester. Its per capita debt has increased almost fourfold. While Syracuse and Onondaga County have remained well below their debt limit as set by New York State, Rochester has kept below its authorized debt ceiling only by resorting to types of bonds that are exempt from the debt limit.

Consequently, items five through seven show that Rochester must now spend almost three times more than Syracuse, per capita, on debt service. The City of Rochester outspends Syracuse on general operations and capital requirements, but Onondaga County government spends more per capita than Monroe County government. As is the case with per capita income, the disparity between Rochester and Monroe County, compared to that between Syracuse and Onondaga County, seems to be increasing. In Rochester, the poor are getting poorer, but their government is spending more and going more into debt.

If Rochester spends more tax dollars per capita than

Table 4

CITY POPULATION AND INCOME AS A PERCENT OF COUNTY POPULATION AND INCOME

	1960	1970	1975
Rochester/Monroe Co.			
Population	54.3	41.4	37.7
Per Capita Income	90.1	84.7	81.6
Syracuse/Onondaga Co.			
Population	51.1	41.7	38.6
Per Capita Income	100.9	93.3	87.9

Syracuse, where is it being spent? As in most cities, the major expenditures are on the large, labor intensive functions such as police, fire, public works, and parks. Syracuse and Rochester spend about the same, per capita, on police and fire. In contrast, almost the entire amount of the discrepancy in per capita expenditures between the two cities is accounted for in public works and debt service expenditures.[21] Rochester is only about one-third larger than Syracuse, but it spends at least twice the amount that Syracuse spends on such activities as building maintenance, street repair, snow and ice control, equipment maintenance, and waste collection and disposal. In some instances, Rochester provides greater services for that extra money, such as in backyard waste collection and sidewalk snowplowing, which Syracuse does not provide. In other cases, Syracuse may be providing services more efficiently.

Technology and Industry

Both Syracuse and Rochester have been shaped significantly by transportation and industrial technology. Both were crossroads of old trade routes and owe their growth in the first half of the nineteenth century to their location as major links on the Erie Canal. Syracuse's position in the center of the state made it a natural "hub" of the rail system. Since World War II, automobile and highway technologies have configured virtually all cities, and Syracuse and Rochester have been no exception. Syracuse, for example, has two major interstate

Table 5

PER CAPITA TAXATION, DEBT, AND EXPENDITURES*

		Monroe	Rochester	Onondaga	Syracuse	NYS Counties Outside NYC
1 Property Tax Authority	1965	82	117	75	109	83
	1974	125	247	102	146	123
2 Property Tax Levied for County(City) Purposes	1965	44	117	42	108	41
	1974	87	242	71	134	82
3 Constitutional Debt Limit	1965	392	462	335	391	389
	1974	551	601	439	481	556
4 Debt **	1965	106	223	84	148	73
	1974	317	808	346	243	272
5 General Current Operations	1965	89	110	84	96	74
	1974	254	255	265	218	262
6 Capital	1965	13	29	37	12	17
	1974	58	137	68	42	42
7 Debt Service	1965	7	69	17	13	11
	1974	31	159	73	63	36
Total	1965	113	217	139	132	109
	1974	369	576	411	309	358

*Based on 1960 and 1970 population.

**Not all debt under New York State law is subject to the state's Constitutional debt limit. In Rochester in 1974, only about 1/2 of its total debt was subject to the debt limit. In Syracuse that year, almost all of the debt was of types subject to the limit.

Source: New York State Department of Audit and Control, Special Report on Municipal Affairs by the State Comptroller, Years ended 1965 and 1974.

highways, Routes 81 and 690, bisecting it. These major roads, combined with inner-city arterials such as the West Street Arterial and Erie Boulevard (built on the bed of the old Erie Canal) provide easy access by car to and from Syracuse and Onondaga County. A collateral effect has been a negative impact on the central city business districts which can now be circumvented by shoppers who can easily drive to suburban shopping areas. Growing suburban populations also support this trend with the construction of more suburban shopping malls.

As transportation technology has affected Syracuse and Rochester, so has industrial technology. In Syracuse, natural brine wells at the foot of Onondaga Lake provided the city with the resources for one of its first industries, the Solvay Process Company. The Allied Chemical Corporation, of which Solvay Process is now a subsidiary, is still dependent upon salt brine deposits in the area for its chemical production. The china manufacturers of Syracuse also use local supply sources. However, most industries are located in the Syracuse area because the general business environment is good for industry.

Syracuse has traditionally been a manufacturing center. One-third of its employment today is in manufacturing (Table 6). With the national growth of industry in the last few decades, some former Syracuse industries have been taken over by large corporations such as General Motors Corporation. Syracuse is also home base for large companies such as Agway, Inc., the Carrier Corporation, and Crouse-Hinds Company. Other firms, such as General Electric, attracted to the area by a good industrial climate (e.g., skilled labor, power, water, transportation, proximity to markets), have chosen to locate plants in the Syracuse area, but their loyalty to the city has declined over the years. As industry has expanded and needed larger facilities, it has spread to industrial parks outside the city limits.[22]

There is enormous diversity in the industries of Syracuse and Onondaga County. Greater Syracuse is represented in all standard industrial categories used in the Census of Manufactures of the U.S. Bureau of the Census. Since there are many large companies in the city and county, no one company plays a dominant role in the overall local economy. Some of these companies such as Bristol Laboratories (pharmaceutical), General Electric, and Carrier could be classified as relatively sophisticated from a technical standpoint.

In addition, Syracuse University influences the general ambience of the city. The university is the third largest employer in the metropolitan area. Syracuse is very much a university town. However, while the financial impact of the university on the community has been measured, the social, political, cultural, or technological impacts are more difficult to assess. There is a discernable "town-gown" division.

Table 6

PERSONAL INCOME FROM WAGES AND SALARIES, 1972
(percent of total, by sector)

	Upstate N.Y.	Monroe	Onondaga
Farms	.3	.1	.1
Contract Construction	6.5	5.8	6.4
Manufacturing	31.1	50.5	30.1
Wholesale and Retail Trade	15.9	12.0	17.7
Finance, Insurance, and Real Estate	3.9	3.5	5.3
Transportation	3.2	1.6	4.3
Communication and Public Utilities	3.2	2.5	4.0
Services	13.4	11.7	13.2
Government	22.2	12.0	18.5
Other	.3	.3	.4

Source: New York State Division of the Budget, New York State Statistical
Yearbook, 1974.

Cooperative ventures of a formal kind between the university
and the city are few. However, informal impacts through
graduates who find employment and individual professors
who consult may be important.

As industrial technology has influenced the evolution of
Syracuse, it has also, perhaps in more striking ways, affected
Rochester. Settlers began to push into western New York at the
close of the Revolutionary War, and people were attracted to
the Rochester area because of the fertile soil and relatively mild
climate influenced by Lake Ontario.[23] The biggest attraction,
however, was the high falls of the Genesee River as it wound its
way to Lake Ontario. Grist mills were soon established. The
soil was ideal for growing wheat, and Rochester began to
emerge as a regional flour center.

The Erie Canal, built between 1817 and 1825, provided access
for the entire nation to be a market for western New York grain,
and Rochester became known as "Flour City," the breadbasket
of the nation. Thus, it was one of the nation's first "boom

towns." When Rochester was incorporated in 1834, it had a population of 12,000 and twenty-one flour mills shipped a million barrels of wheat each year.

By 1850, the Midwest had eclipsed the Rochester region in the production of flour, and Rochester, with a population of 36,000, began to diversify. The fertile soil and mild climate encouraged a large seed and nursery industry. German immigrants also established Rochester as a thriving shoe and clothing center.

Rochester's basic industrial pattern was set in the late 1800s by a number of inventors. Chief among them was George Eastman, whose experiments in his mother's kitchen led to the eventual development of a flexible, paper-based film to replace glass photographic plates. In the 1880s, Eastman produced the first small box camera intended for the mass market. Photography became more and more popular. Eastman enhanced his company's position by acquiring useful and potentially conflicting patents, and photographic inventions streamed from Rochester. By 1927, Eastman Kodak employed 7,000 people and had its own industrial park consisting of 120 buildings.

The influence on Rochester of Eastman and the company he founded is incalculable. Until his death in 1932, George Eastman himself towered over most aspects of life in Rochester. He heavily endowed the University of Rochester and the Rochester Institute of Technology. He built up the Chamber of Commerce and the local YMCA. He established the renowned Eastman School of Music and built a magnificent Eastman Theater. He also spurred government reform by establishing a Bureau of Municipal Research.

Throughout the twentieth century, Eastman Kodak has dominated employment in Rochester. With current employment at about 52,000, Kodak provides about one-third of all manufacturing jobs in the five-county Rochester area and, roughly, one-eighth of employment of all types. Each spring, the local economy receives a boost when Eastman Kodak distributes wage bonuses to its employees. Recently, these bonuses have reached about $100 million annually.

Other Rochester industries are also based on high technology. Xerox Corporation, whose precursor began in Rochester about 1900, now employs approximately 15,000 people in Monroe County. Most of the growth of this corporation occurred after the development of xerography in 1960. Bausch and Lomb, makers of optical equipment and lenses, began as the small shop of two nineteenth-century German immigrants. Sybron Corporation produces Taylor instruments and Ritter dental equipment. General Motors employs about 9,000 in Monroe County at its Delco Division, which manufactures carburetors. The generally good economic health of the Rochester area recently has thus been due to a dependence on industries that have been prosperous, especially those related to photography, office copiers, and automobiles.

As in Syracuse/Onondaga County, rapid suburbanization occurred in Rochester/Monroe County during the 1950s and 1960s. This included industry as well as housing and retail outlets. Kodak has expanded into the adjacent suburban town of Greece. Xerox moved its principal manufacturing plant to neighboring Webster in 1958. Graflex and Strasenburgh, two other large employers in the Rochester area also moved to the suburbs in the late 1950s. As these industries prospered during the 1960s, the stage was set for the rapid population growth of Monroe County, which occurred outside the city of Rochester. As in Syracuse, the turning point came around 1960 when, for the first time, more assessed property valuation was found outside than inside the city.

The high-technology climate of Rochester is supplemented by the presence of two technically strong academic institutions. The University of Rochester, though not as large as Syracuse University in terms of student population, is one of the most heavily endowed universities in the nation, with Eastman and other Rochester industrialists being the major benefactors. The university is well-regarded for its basic research, especially in medicine and optics. Rochester Institute of Technology is a nationally known engineering school. In the late 1960s, it moved to a new $50 million campus on the outskirts of Rochester. Joseph Wilson, of Xerox Corporation, was a prime benefactor.

Hence it can be seen that both Syracuse and Rochester have

had a long relationship with technology, primarily on the private sector side. Recently, there have been conscious attempts to use technology to improve public services in these two cities.

Politics

A clear-cut trend in political party competition has developed in both Syracuse and Rochester in the past decade. In both metropolitan areas, one-party dominance in local politics has been replaced by rather fierce two-party competition. As late as 1960, there were few Democratic office holders in Monroe and Onondaga Counties. Indeed, some of the rural towns had never elected a Democrat to any local public office. By contrast, in the wake of the November 1977 local elections, Democrats gained control of the Onondaga and Monroe county legislatures. This is the first time Democrats have ever been in power in Onondaga County, and only the second time in Monroe County. Democrats also control the two city halls.

The recent success of Democrats may be surprising, given party enrollment figures (Table 7). Since the Civil War, enrolled Republicans have always outnumbered enrolled Democrats in the two areas, and this is still the case. However, the power of Republicans seems clearly to be on the wane. Republicans lost about 8 percent of their enrollment in Rochester and Monroe County in the past decade and lost only slightly less in Syracuse and Onondaga County. The trends for both upstate New York and the entire state have not been as dramatic.

Republican losses have been absorbed almost equally in both areas by the Democratic party and the ranks of independents. Today, Rochester and Monroe County are slightly more Democratic than Syracuse and Onondaga County, while the latter have more independent voters. As the gap between the number of Republicans and Democrats continues to narrow, the growth of independents may in the near future deny both main parties a majority of enrolled voters. Also, the organizational strength of political parties has been hurt by decreasing access to patronage jobs and the replacement of

Table 7

PARTY ENROLLMENT*

(percent of total enrollment)

	Republican 1966	1974	Democratic 1966	1974	Independent 1966	1974
Monroe County	63.8	56.1	28.8	31.0	6.5	10.6
Rochester	55.9	47.2	36.2	40.1	7.0	10.5
Onondaga County	60.8	54.6	27.1	27.9	11.0	15.1
Syracuse	58.4	50.7	28.5	31.9	12.1	15.6
New York State	39.0	37.7	50.4	49.2	8.6	9.9
New York State (excluding New York City)	54.1	50.8	34.5	35.5	10.0	10.9

*1966 and 1974 were chosen for comparison because both were years of gubernatorial elections in New York. Enrollments increase in presidential election years and decrease in off-election years.

Source: New York State Department of State. Legislative Manual, 1968, 1976.

county boards of supervisors with county legislatures. The parties must now be content with fewer loyal followers and less influence on public policy.

Aside from changes in enrollment, can anything be said about the "ideological climate" of the two areas? In the twentieth century, under the leadership of both Republican and Democratic governors and state legislatures, New York State has gained a "liberal" reputation in areas of social welfare policy. However, this tendency has not been evenly diffused geographically. As if to balance "ultraliberal" New York City, upstate counties have generally been considered fiscally and socially conservative. Metropolitan Syracuse and Rochester have shared this upstate image. Despite these stereotypes, however, it can be argued, on the basis of recent gubernatorial elections, that Rochester tends to be politically more liberal than Syracuse (Table 8). Since 1966, Syracuse has consistently given much less of its vote to the candidate for governor with a liberal image than has Rochester. (In 1966, Rockefeller, a Republican, had a liberal image. In 1970 and 1974, Arthur Goldberg and Hugh Carey, both Democrats, had liberal

Table 8

PERCENT OF TOTAL
VOTE CAST FOR GOVERNOR BY PARTY

	1966		1970		1974	
	R	D	R	D	R	D
New York State	44	37	51	35	35	51
Upstate	48	35	54	33	41	47
Monroe County	45	36	47	36	38	52
Rochester	40	44	43	43	31	58
Onondaga County	33	49	51	31	51	37
Syracuse	33	52	49	35	46	42

R = Republican   D = Democrat

images.) The suburbs in both areas tend to be more conservative than the cities.

Government

As Syracuse and Rochester have relatively similar political climates, they also have governments that have much in common. Indeed, in thinking about the Syracuse and Rochester areas governmentally, it is useful to consider four governmental systems: Syracuse, Onondaga County, Rochester, and Monroe County. These four governments sponsor most public services in the greater Syracuse and Rochester areas.

Syracuse

In fiscal year 1977, Syracuse had a budget of approximately $59 million; an additional $51 million went to support the city's public schools. Presiding over the bulk of these expenditures is a "strong" mayor. All departments except education report to the mayor, but even education is indirectly under the authority of the mayor.

The Syracuse School District, headed by an appointed superintendent, is governed by a seven-member board of education elected at large, but its budget is subject to review by the city board of estimate composed of the mayor, the president of the Syracuse Common Council, and the director of finance (an appointee of the mayor). The school district budget also must be approved by the full council.

The power of the mayor is checked by a common council with customary legislative powers. The common council consists of a president and four members elected at large, together with five others elected by district. Bonding resolutions, a primary means for funding large-scale technologies, must be passed by a two-thirds vote of the council.

Lee Alexander was elected mayor of Syracuse in 1969 and was reelected in 1977 for a third term. Alexander was the first Democratic mayor in many years and has had a Democratic-controlled council with which to work. However, the local Democratic party is far from unified, and the Democrats on the council have been rather independent, not fearing to oppose mayoral programs and budgets on occasion.

Although the mayor in Syracuse is a strong mayor, Alexander has chosen not to become too involved in the daily operations of city government. When he was first elected, many politicos predicted that the young, photogenic mayor would soon be seeking higher office. After he was re-elected for a second term, he decided to run for the U.S. Senate. Although he was backed by the state Democratic party, he was easily defeated in the Democratic primary by activist Ramsey Clark. Undaunted, Alexander shifted his attention from higher elected office to professional activities, expending much of his energy on the U.S. Conference of Mayors. In 1977, he was elected its president, the first representing a small-to-medium-sized city.

Understandably, all of these outside activities have cut into the time that Alexander personally spends on city business. To govern the city, Alexander has, from the beginning of his administration, delegated broad authority to his department heads. By and large, his appointments have been based more on professional reputation, experience, and ability than on patronage or partisanship. For example, his commissioner of finance is a Republican holdover from the previous administration and is regarded as a master of municipal finance who has helped keep the city in a relatively strong financial position. Thus, it can be said that Alexander has created a

climate that very much encourages independence and professionalism in his city agencies.

At the same time, Alexander's outside contacts have also paid
dividends. He has tried to ensure that his agencies would not
have to face austerity programs through reliance on the city's
dwindling tax base. To obtain outside funds, he not only has
personally spent a great deal of time pursuing federal grants in
Washington, but he has also built a powerful new office in city
hall to garner federal and state funds: the Office of Federal and
State Aid Coordination. Syracuse now relies on federal and
state funds for about 30 percent of its budget. In contrast,
Rochester, in fiscal year 1977, derived only about 16 percent of
its budget from state and federal aid.

Onondaga County

In fiscal year 1976, the budget of Onondaga County was $222
million. A breakdown of city and county budgets by function is
shown in Table 9. The general governmental organization of
the county is comparable to that of Syracuse. This similarity
points up the effects of the county's urbanization. Since the
beginning of the 1960s, the county has modernized its
governmental operations. In 1961, the town-oriented Board of
Supervisors of Onondaga County that had served as both the
executive and legislative branches was supplemented by an
elected county executive with authority over administrative
departments. In 1966, the effect of population changes and
related reapportionment cases continued the modernization
trend when the board of supervisors was replaced by the current
county legislature. The county was reapportioned and divided
into twenty-four legislative districts with equal populations:
twelve within the city and twelve outside the city. In effect,
county government also has a "strong-mayor" type of government. Budget procedures for both units are similar, except that
the county legislature can make line-item adjustments which
the city council cannot do.

Power relationships between city and county have been shifting slowly toward the county, in terms of control over new
(and some old) functions. A number of social service and

Table 9

BUDGETS OF THE CITY OF SYRACUSE
AND ONONDAGA COUNTY
(in thousands $)

City of Syracuse, Fiscal Year 1977		County of Onondaga, Fiscal Year 1976	
Council	$ 89	Legislative	$ 305
Judiciary Dept.	593	Executive	195
Executive	418	Staff	9,690
Dept. of Finance	364	Judicial	4,771
Dept. of Audit	87	Public Safety	4,521
License Commission	30	Correction	4,260
City Clerk	69	Drainage and Sanitation	17,433
Dept. of Purchase	190	Highways	11,516
Dept. of Assessment	275	Water	6,824
Dept. of Law	257	Special Activities	721
Consumer Affairs	70	Mental Health	6,005
Dept. of Engineering	437	Health	12,477
Board of Elections	173	Social Services	88,985
Dept. of Community Dev.	386	Education	9,683
Dept. of Public Works	5,567	Libraries	2,502
Dept. of Fire	8,828	Recreation	2,592
Dept. of Police	8,870	Natural Resources	80
Dept. of Transporation	2,704	Other--Aging	121
Dept. of Parks & Recreation	2,453	Other--Auth. Agencies	2,648
Dept. of Aviation	1,426	Other--County General	28,063
Special Objects of Expense	14,598	Other--Gen. Fnd. Dbt. Sv.	6,329
Debt Service	3,122	Fed. Rev. Fund Debt Sv.	2,454
Capital Appropriation	2,949		
Tax Reserve	70		
Bureau of Water	3,815		
Bureau of Sewers	727		
Downtown Fund	400		
Total	$58,967	Total	$222,175

welfare programs, formerly left to the city and small towns, have been taken over by the county. In 1967, public health, once a city responsibility, became a county function. Environmental quality has come under county jurisdiction. The city and smaller governments have not been able to afford the costs of the services that were transferred. More recently, data processing, the city zoo, the city library system, and solid waste disposal have been added to the list of functions being transferred from city jurisdiction.

In the process of acquiring new services mandated by federal and state laws, the county has also grown as a regulator. As noted in a report by the League of Women Voters:

There has been the transfer to county government of some traditional regulatory powers of town, village, and city governments. For example, Onondaga County has a uniform County Plumbing Code, a County Health Department (which enforces the county and state sanitary codes), and a County Planning Agency (combined with the city), which has some influence over local zoning decisions.[24]

The most notable observation on the Onondaga County governmental process is that most of these vast changes in county government since 1961 have been overseen by a single chief executive, County Executive John Mulroy. A farm owner who was previously the supervisor of a rural town, Republican Mulroy has been the county's first and only county executive, reputedly the longest reigning county chief executive in the nation.

Until January 1978, Mulroy had a Republican-dominated county legislature with which to work, and this combination provided relative stability and predictability in county government operations. In contrast to Mayor Alexander, Mulroy is an insider who oversees every detail of county government management. While many of his department heads are competent professionals, such as nationally known county engineer John Hennigan, it cannot be said that Mulroy delegates much responsibility or gives free rein to his line officers. On the other hand, Mulroy is regarded as a political progressive who, while maintaining the highest possible rating for county bonds, has steered county government toward growth and the acquisition of increased responsibilities.

Rochester

In fiscal year 1977, Rochester's budget stood at about $132.4 million, excluding education. In charge of these expenditures is a city manager. Rochester adopted the council-manager form of government in 1928, and was one of the first large cities to do so. The change in government was a classic example of the "good government" movement of the early 1900s. George Eastman's Bureau of Municipal Research was a strong influence, but the adoption of the new form of government would not have occurred had it not been for a bitter intraparty split in the local Republican party. Party leaders, both Democratic and Republican, were opposed to the change in the structure of government and attempted to overturn the decision of the voters in court. Although the council-manager form of government was upheld, the court struck down nonpartisan city elections.

The relationship between partisan elections and the city manager has been a continuing issue in Rochester politics. Whether or not the council-manager form of government has brought professional administration to Rochester, or at least more professionalism than in cities without it is certainly open to question. Since 1928, there have been 13 city managers who have had an average tenure of less than four years each.[25] Although one manager in the 1940s held this position for thirteen years, many others stayed only a very short time, probably making the establishment of routinized management procedures very difficult. Whenever party control changed at city hall, the manager was sure to go. The same often held true when the leadership of the party in control changed. Partisan influence over city managers was maintained, moreover, by choosing most managers from in-house candidates. Some of the early managers were civil engineers, but only Porter Homer, in the early 1960s, and the current manager, Elisha Freedman, have been professionally trained public administrators.

The drawbacks of Rochester's council-manager government have been pointed out in a recent proposal for a new Rochester charter.[26] For example, it has been difficult to make long-range decisions. The nine-member city council often becomes involved in administrative decisions, including personnel and labor relations. Policy has tended to be made in reaction to crises. Councilmen have held informal veto power over departmental appointments even though the manager, in theory, has full authority. The policy-making tension between the manager and the council has, in addition, not been ameliorated by the mayor, who has few official duties other than presiding over the council.[27] In sum, one study of Rochester's government concludes:

The council-manager system as it exists in Rochester has a substantial weakness in that there is no unified policy leadership. The position of mayor, as presently constituted, does not provide the power necessary for strong policy leadership. Further, the fragmented council, with its members reacting differentially to pressures, events, and individual motivations, has not provided a stable basis of support to the manager for constructive longer-range programs or quality administration. . . . The city manager is in the difficult position of having his efforts divided on both administration and policy—with insufficient time to spend on either function.[28]

In spite of these limitations, Elisha Freedman, who became city manager in 1974, has sought and been accorded increased authority, especially in making appointments. For example, he convened a panel of respected fire chiefs to interview candidates for the city's fire chief position. The International Association of Chiefs of Police, similarly, was consulted on the selection of a police chief. Freedman also began an overhaul of Rochester's Department of Public Works (DPW), which was generally conceded to be inefficiently operated and bloated by patronage. Employment in the DPW has now been reduced by nearly one-half.

At least part of the reason for the recent ability of the city manager to play a larger role is the decline in the power of organized political parties. As noted earlier, Monroe County voters have not remained loyal to their party candidates. Moreover, patronage jobs have steadily given way to civil service appointments, and the importance of "ward politics" has been eclipsed, a victim of legislative district reapportionment. Party politics appears to have given way to the politics of issues, and interest groups in Rochester have replaced political parties as the major political actors. "Neighborhood associations and special interest groups are playing a larger role in decision-making than has previously been the case," a recent study concluded.[29] For example, a group of neighborhood organizations that formed the South East Area Coalition was instrumental in blocking the construction of the Genesee Expressway, a proposed major intraurban superhighway. Rochester, to a greater degree than Syracuse, has a number of strong interest groups ranging from a politically active chamber of commerce to ethnic and neighborhood-centered associations.

Monroe County

In fiscal year 1976, Monroe County's budget was about $284 million (see Table 10 for a comparison of the budgets of Rochester and Monroe County). This money was funneled through a government organization that resembled that of Rochester in certain respects. Following the lead of Rochester, Monroe County appointed a county manager in 1936. At that time, the county's legislative body was the board of supervisors, and county managers tended to be chosen from the ranks of the supervisors. Unlike the city manager, however, the county manager was appointed for a four-year term. In 1965, the board of supervisors was replaced by a county legislature, divided into twenty-nine legislative districts of which twelve are located in Rochester. The manager currently is Lucien Morin, a former town official who became manager in 1972.

The county manager has always been subject to intense partisan pressure and has had difficulty in providing independent leadership. In the county, governmental leadership has usually been exercised by either the county Republican chairman or by the legislative majority leader.

Political pressures notwithstanding, there has been a long-standing trend toward consolidation of urban functions at the county level in Monroe County. Indeed, Monroe County has been a leader in New York State in this regard. While the growth of county control over former city functions did not begin until the 1960s in Onondaga County, transfer of functions from city to county government have been occurring in Monroe County since the 1940s. At an earlier time and to a greater extent than Onondaga County, Monroe County has become a metropolitan government. It is increasingly difficult to discuss Rochester city functions without reference to county government.

Other Governments

City and county are not the only important governments in

Table 10

BUDGETS OF THE CITY OF ROCHESTER
AND MONROE COUNTY
(in thousands $)

City of Rochester,Fiscal Year 1977*		County of Monroe, Fiscal Year 1976	
Council, Clerk	$ 427	Legislature	$ 600
Mayor	104	Staff	2,616
Courts	821	Finance	2,141
City Manager	131	Planning	821
Budget	367	Elections	1,442
Personnel	376	County Clerk	1,793
Labor Relations	70	Public Works	16,763
Public Information	191	Judicial	11,442
Data Processing	781	Public Safety	7,740
Law	592	Correction	5,090
Program Development	472	Social Services	140,120
Dept. of Finance	1,833	Mental Health	5,197
Bldgs. & Property Conserv.	2,052	Public Health	9,974
Community Development	3,945	Education	5,571
Parks and Recreation	5,849	Libraries	3,438
Dept. of Fire	12,535	Recreation	6,748
Dept. of Police	13,738	Public Enterprise	3,093
Library	3,552	Pure Waters	35,831
Dept. of Public Works	27,935	Economic Opportunity	575
Equipment & Facilities	4,350	Authorized Agencies	1,300
Undistributed Expenses	24,230	Special Expense	21,351
Contingent	175		
Debt Service	26,388		
Tax Reserve	2,844		
Less: Credits	-1,349		
Total	$132,407	Total	$283,646

*Note: Rochester's fiscal year 1977 began July 1, 1976. Fiscal year
1977 began in Syracuse on January 1, 1977.

metropolitan Syracuse and Rochester. There are over 700 other
governmental units in Onondaga County, including 15
villages, 19 towns, 654 special town districts, 18 school districts,
23 county districts, 5 public authorities, and 5 urban renewal
agencies. The number of governmental units in Monroe
County is comparable. There are many towns that were once
rural but are now essentially extensions of the two cities. Most
of these are governed, as they have been in the past, by town
boards that are reluctant to make changes. However, the
demand for more sophisticated services has increasingly caused

them to consider modernization. As the difference between these towns and the city diminish, their fears of acquiring social problems similar to those of the city increase. They worry about becoming embroiled in the problems of the city, some of which have racial overtones. They identify with the county, although their bucolic image is more a relic of nostalgia than a vision of their future.

Units of government known as "public authorities" require special comment. These exist in such fields as housing (New York Urban Development Corporation), mass transit (regional authorities), solid waste (county-wide authorities), and other functions. They are major actors in the governance of Syracuse and Rochester. To whom are they accountable? The city? The county? It is not at all clear. They exist in a quasi-public, quasi-private interjurisdictional status. With organizations such as these playing comprehensive roles in key functional areas, it is difficult for the principal elected officials to be as strong in fact as they are in theory. Contributing to the fragmentation of power and the local or "horizontal" perspective on urban technology is the fact that key functional areas in Syracuse and Rochester, as in other American cities, vary greatly in terms of their intergovernmental or "vertical" relations. Some agencies (police, transportation) have counterparts in federal government that provide them with funds in addition to those they receive locally. Other agencies (fire) are not so benefited. Such vertical governmental systems produce centrifugal forces on agencies that make them appear often to have more important linkages with Albany and Washington than with "central coordinators" such as a mayor, city manager, or county executive.

Conclusion

Greater Syracuse and Rochester have been discussed as a setting for local public services. This setting highlights the dilemmas of governmental fragmentation, of burgeoning problems, of administrative mechanisms geared to political jurisdictions outmoded by population shifts. The fragmentation of jurisdiction has the effect of dividing authority sufficiently to keep any overarching local "power elite" from emerging. There is no metropolitan-wide or even city-wide governing elite. Indeed, in many areas, there appears to be no central coordination either at the city or county level, except in extremely unusual circumstances. There is certainly no metropolitan-wide coordination. More often than not, there is rivalry within the system.

Where political power is weak, distracted, indifferent, or divided, bureaucratic power has filled the vacuum in urban service management to some extent. Various islands of functional authority have been established within the system. The overall trend is toward allowing professionalized bureaucracies to make decisions with varying degrees of accountability and autonomy. What is true for decision making in urban services generally is true for decisions involving innovation. In the absence of central coordinators with the power base to plan innovation in ways that are comprehensive, bureaucratic and special interest power holds sway. To the extent that agencies are innovation oriented, or pressed to be so by a politically active clientele, their decisions may "bubble up" and become the choices of the locality. Innovation thus occurs unevenly among the public service areas, determined less by the specific characteristics of the city than the dynamics of a particular public service arena and the entrepreneurial capacities of a given agency.

Topside officials do matter, insofar as creating a climate for change is concerned. The general history, economic base, industrial flavor, and population characteristics of the city also contribute to the overall climate for innovation. Undoubtedly, they set the boundaries for what is possible in a given service area. However, within these boundaries, there is considerable room for initiative. Where specifics are concerned, we have to go beneath the surface features of the cities to the organizations and individuals who are concerned with public service delivery on a day-to-day basis. It is with them that most urban innovations begin and end.

3

Case Histories of Innovations

The data base on which the analysis is drawn consists of twenty comparative case histories of local government innovations in the Syracuse and Rochester metropolitan areas. Some are complete innovations in the sense that they involve adoption, implementation, and incorporation into the routines of a local function. However, many are incomplete. The incomplete, or nonincorporated, innovations may be rejected at the adoption stage. They may be adopted but not implemented. Sometimes, they can be incorporated in a very limited way, i.e., used in a manner that suggests they are nice to have but not essential in public service delivery.

The selection of cases was aimed at exploring a range of experience in local government innovation over the past decade. The cases were chosen following a thorough reconnaissance based on interviews with people knowledgeable about public services in Syracuse and Rochester, both in and out of local government. In addition, newspapers and other secondary sources were searched for instances of technological innovation decision making by local government. Finally, the candidate cases were screened on the basis of such criteria as:

1. coverage of a range of urban functions;
2. inclusion of cases both in Syracuse and Rochester and the larger metropolitan regions of these cities;
3. range of types (hardware and managerial techniques);
4. range of costs;
5. range of completion along the continuum from adoption to incorporation; and

6. national significance; the innovations had to be important to Syracuse and Rochester and also be the kinds of innovations being introduced to other cities in the country.

Initially, we had intended to prepare fourteen cases as a basis for analysis. In the process of performing the research, we uncovered additional cases judged useful for inclusion. For example, instead of writing one case in the police field in Syracuse, we prepared two; instead of one case on solid waste disposal in Onondaga County, we wrote two. We felt it would be extremely helpful in understanding the particular functional or bureaucratic setting of innovation if we had more than one innovative experience from which to generalize in certain instances. Consequently, instead of producing the fourteen cases we originally planned, we have twenty. Fourteen are from Syracuse, and six are from Rochester. There is comparison among functions in each city and between functions in the two cities.

From these cases, we have attempted the analysis in the succeeding chapters. In this chapter, we summarize the cases. The cases in full are available as part of the report submitted to the National Science Foundation, on which this book is based. The complete cases covered events up to September 1976 in Syracuse and September 1977 in Rochester, at which time the report was finalized for the National Science Foundation. However, in the following case summaries, we have included significant events affecting the outcomes of the cases up to September 1978.

EDUCATION

Project Unique in Rochester

Project Unique was a large-scale, federally funded set of innovations designed to address the problems of reducing racial imbalance and improving urban education in the Rochester city schools. It was composed of nine programmatic components including, in part: a downtown classroom with technological teaching aids; a magnet elementary school; a teacher internship program; SPAN (School Parent Advisors to the Neighborhood program); a community resources council; and RISE (Right of an Individual to Secure an Education program). Initial plans also included the construction of a large educational complex and an 800-pupil magnet school linked with a centralized district educational administration office. However, programmatic rather than capital innovations were emphasized in the application for Office of Education Title III funding.

The concept of Project Unique was developed by a coalition of the Rochester City School District, the University of Rochester, the Eastman Kodak Company, and the Industrial Management Council. The superintendent of the Rochester City School District served as bureaucratic entrepreneur from the initial planning stage to implementation. A full proposal of twelve innovative programs was developed with a planning grant from the Elementary and Secondary Education Act in 1966-1967. From 1967 to 1970, Project Unique received over $4.5 million in federal funding to implement nine of the twelve program components. Upon termination of federal support in 1970, some of the components were eliminated, some were modified, and only two (the magnet elementary school and the urban-suburban transfer program) were incorporated.

The study of Project Unique provides information on the vital process of coalition building for successful implementation of educational innovation. The broad membership of the coalitions changed at each stage, with continuity in some key roles, particularly that of the bureaucratic entrepreneur. The availability of federal funds is also significant. Without them, Project Unique would perhaps have been smaller in scale and scope, probably a cooperative project between the city school district and the University of Rochester.

Project Unique was an incremental rather than radical set of innovations in that (1) it had the capacity to be modified as it was being implemented; (2) it was separable into program components; and, (3) if it later proved to be unsuccessful, it could be reversed because of the small investment in capital improvement. It was the separability factor which allowed

several components to be dropped, others to be changed, and
two to be institutionalized after federal funding was terminated.

Campus Plan in Syracuse

In the mid-1960s, Syracuse was faced with two educational
problems: the need to integrate the school system racially and
to replace obsolete school buildings. Campus Plan was an
educational park concept proposed by the superintendent of
the Syracuse City School District and members of his staff as a
solution to these problems, as well as an improvement in the
quality of education in the city schools. This plan would have
replaced the existing elementary schools in the city (grades
kindergarten through sixth) with four campuses located in
four quadrants of the city. Each campus would have contained
eight schools plus central facilities. It would have provided
many sophisticated, technological innovations in individually
programmed instruction. The pupils would have been bused to
the campuses.

From its inception in 1966, Campus Plan was extremely
controversial. It never went beyond the planning stage, but the
planning stage itself was lengthy and turbulent. Over the next
three years, the superintendent of schools acted as entrepreneur
and obtained federal funds to conduct three feasibility studies
in support of the plan.

Opponents objected to eliminating the neighborhood
schools, the busing of young children far from home, the
innovative technology which they feared would replace
teachers with machines, and what they considered the
prohibitive expense to the city, not only to build the campuses
but also to operate them after they were completed. Adoption
costs of the first campus, with a 4270-pupil capacity, would
have been $19.7 million in capital costs, plus a 40 percent
increase in the annual operating budget, which amounted to a
$1.07 million increase yearly. Full incorporation of four
campuses would have required a minimum of $75 million in
capital costs plus a 40 percent increase in operating costs, or
a $4.28 million increase annually.

Initially, the mayor of Syracuse gave support to the concept. But, as the controversy grew, he became silent. The superintendent made no effort to form coalitions of political or general public support. He depended upon the technical information of his feasibility studies to convince the Syracuse Board of Education of the merits of the plan.

In fall 1968, the superintendent submitted a six-part resolution on Campus Plan to the board of education. At a special meeting on October 28, 1968, the board of education tabled the first three parts of the resolution having to do with its approval of the plan for adoption pending the results of action on the last three parts. Of these last three parts the first two dealt with authorization of the superintendent to seek funding from outside sources to be used for capital construction and operating expenses of the plan, and the third authorized him to arrange public hearings on the issue.

The superintendent was unable to obtain the necessary outside funding to implement the plan if it were adopted. The board of education held public hearings on January 9 and 10, 1969, but positions were not changed as a result of these hearings. By summer 1969, Campus Plan was a dead issue.

FIRE PROTECTION

The Mini-Pumper in Rochester

A mini-pumper is a small, two-man fire truck specially equipped to fight minor fires. In Rochester, it was seen as part of the solution to the Rochester Fire Department's financial problems of the early 1970s. The departmental budget had risen rapidly because of wage and benefit increases. Then, in 1974, the budget was further increased when the department was forced to add thirty-one firefighters to its force to comply with a state-mandated, forty-hour work week. At this point, the city manager directed the fire chief to search for ways to cut costs.

After reading journal articles about the mini-pumper and talking with the Syracuse fire chief whose department had been using mini-pumpers since 1972, the Rochester fire chief and his staff decided to purchase one mini-pumper to replace a standard fire pumper due for replacement. The mini-pumper would allow the fire department to decrease the staff by twelve men, saving the department an estimated $300,000 annually, and the $29,000 cost of the mini-pumper would fall within the departmental budget.

There was no opposition to the adoption of the mini-pumper; however, at the implementation stage, the firemen's union tried to prevent its use. The union's campaign against the mini-pumper culminated in a public debate between union and management officials. However, no strong public opposition formed, and the implementation proceeded. The mini-pumper is now introduced into the Rochester Fire Department. The union accepted this one defeat but vowed to fight again if future acquisitions were to occur. At the time of this writing, no further adoptions of the mini-pumper were proceeding.

The Mini-Pumper in Syracuse

In Syracuse, as in Rochester, the fire department was facing financial problems in the early 1970s. In addition to the budgeting problem brought about by the state-mandated, forty-hour work week, the Syracuse Fire Department had substandard facilities and inadequate equipment which needed replacing and updating. To solve these combined problems, there was an overall reorganization of the Syracuse Fire Department, with the department acquiring new equipment as part of the modernization effort. The mini-pumper, a small, two-man fire truck specially equipped to fight minor fires, was the most radical of the proposed changes. The decision to adopt and implement the mini-pumper was made because it enabled the department to respond flexibly to various demands. It also permitted the department to use manpower and equipment more productively. During the first full year of operation, mini-pumpers responded to 48 percent of all alarms.

The fire chief, acting as entrepreneur, won the support of the mayor, the city council, the firefighters, and the news media. The favorable interaction of the fire chief with these actors had a strong, positive effect on the momentum of the decision-making process from adoption to incorporation. An important contributing factor to implementation was the cooperation and proximity of the manufacturer. The firefighters actually participated in the design of the vehicle by a local firm. This helped to increase their acceptance of the mini-pumper. Union opposition to this innovation was not a factor in Syracuse, in part because of the manner in which the fire chief conducted its implementation. A potential threat to its incorporation was the decision of the Insurance Rating Office to deny credit to the mini-pumper for insurance purposes. Later, this decision was reversed.

The mini-pumper has been incorporated into the Syracuse Fire Department. The department purchased twelve vehicles at a total cost of $264,000. On a department-wide basis, this investment is expected to yield $1,176,000 in equipment savings over a fifteen-year period and $492,000 in manpower savings annually.

Uniform Fire Incident Reporting System (UFIRS) in Syracuse

UFIRS is a computer-assisted management information system for the collection of standard data to help fire department officials plan more effective ways to utilize firefighting resources to prevent and suppress fires.

The Syracuse fire chief, as part of his plan to improve the Syracuse Fire Department in the early 1970s, recognized the need for such a computerized data processing system and asked the newly-appointed department analyst to develop one. Shortly after starting on this project, the analyst discovered that the National Fire Protection Association (NFPA), funded by the federal Department of Housing and Urban Development, had developed UFIRS and was ready to market it at a fraction of what it would have cost the analyst to develop his system.

Upon the recommendation of the analyst, the Syracuse Fire Department decided to adopt UFIRS. The actual adoption was delayed for a time because UFIRS was designed for a different computer system than that used in Onondaga County. The fire department did not want the expense of converting NFPA's system to fit the requirements of the Onondaga County Data Processing Department, and NFPA refused to reduce the cost of

UFIRS enough to defray this expense. Eventually, as the analyst had hoped, there was sufficient demand for UFIRS by other fire departments with the same problem. NFPA then made the necessary adaptive changes in its system, and the Syracuse Fire Department bought it at an initial cost of $2500.

During the implementation stage, the analyst was an invaluable link between the fire department and the Syracuse Data Processing Bureau. He had left the fire department to work with the data processing bureau and continued to be helpful in installing the new system. However, he later left the bureau before all of the implementation problems had been solved. As there was no one to fill his role, the analyst continued to consult with the city to incorporate the innovation. Given the firm commitment of the fire department to the incorporation of UFIRS, it seemed certain that someone would be found to fill the role of liaison between the Syracuse Fire Department and the Syracuse Data Processing Bureau.

Rapid Water in Syracuse

Rapid Water is a chemical additive that speeds the flow of water through fire hoses, thus increasing the amount of water firefighters can apply to a fire in a given amount of time. Its use is often seen as justifying a reduction in manpower of one man per pumper.

Rand and Union Carbide developed the process, using the New York City Fire Department for demonstration purposes. Impressed by the successful testing of the product by the New York City Fire Department, the Syracuse fire chief wished to include Rapid Water in his modernization effort and contacted Union Carbide to arrange for a local demonstration. After the demonstration, Rapid Water was adopted, and plans were made for its implementation.

Although the implementation of Rapid Water had met with union opposition in New York City, the only opposition in Syracuse came from the older firefighters who objected to the special training required to utilize it. The fire chief quickly solved this problem by assigning its use to companies with predominantly younger men who were enthusiastic about modernization of their department. As the older firefighters retired, their places would be filled by men who had the necessary training, and this problem would be permanently solved.

Rapid Water has been incorporated into the Syracuse Fire Department. The initial acquisition costs over a three-year period were $50,000. Because of its expense, its use has been limited to serious fires in which life is in danger and those less serious fires in which property can be salvaged.

Optical Communication (OPTICOM) in Syracuse

OPTICOM is a system employing an electronic device that enables an approaching emergency vehicle to switch a red traffic light to green and keep it green until the vehicle has passed through the intersection. It was perfected and marketed by the 3M Company.

The Syracuse fire chief wanted OPTICOM included in the modernization plan because, in addition to promoting highway safety, it would allow speedier responses by fire trucks. If the OPTICOM system, with this time-saving feature, were installed throughout the city at every intersection having a traffic signal, the fire chief believed that it would be possible to enlarge the area covered by each fire company. As a result, two fire companies could eventually be eliminated in the future construction of fire stations. The elimination of the two companies would reduce his total force by forty-one fire-fighters. The resulting savings in capital costs and manpower would more than offset the $640,000 needed to install OPTICOM. As economic feasibility was an issue in adoption, funding was obtained from the federal and state departments of transportation which cosponsored a two-year demonstration of OPTICOM for use by both the police and fire departments. At the end of this demonstration period, the police department decided not to join the fire department in its request for the acquisition of OPTICOM. The fire chief, however, convinced the Syracuse Common Council of the merits of OPTICOM, and bids were received from the 3M Company and the Rad-O-Lite Company, a newcomer to the field. Rad-O-Lite had the lower bid, but the fire chief preferred the 3M system. Therefore, the contract was awarded to the 3M Company, and implementation was begun.

The implementation stage was complicated by two factors. First, the fire chief had underestimated the cost of installation and the time it would consume. Second, a law suit was brought by Rad-O-Lite challenging the contract award to the 3M Company on the grounds that it did not meet certain New York State Department of Transportation traffic regulations.

When this case study was written in fall 1976, the matter was still under litigation. However, the city was proceeding to complete the installation of the 3M system pending the legal outcome. Also, in 1976, to expedite installation, three full-time union electricians were hired by the fire department for the sole purpose of installing the system. Such work had been performed previously by in-house Syracuse Department of Transportation personnel who could only manage an average of one installation per day. Installation took much longer to complete than originally estimated, even with the full-time union electricians, and legal skirmishes delayed the final implementation of OPTICOM.

HOUSING

Industrialized Housing in Rochester

Industrialized housing employed two techniques of European origin for constructing high-rise apartment complexes. Although the designs differed, each specified using large component parts (i.e., concrete slabs) to be made in a factory and delivered to the construction site for assembly.

In the 1960s, there had been a major population shift from the city of Rochester to the suburbs and an influx into the city of low-income and minority groups who had need for low-income public housing. In 1970, the New York State Urban Development Corporation (UDC) started to work with Rochester to solve its housing problems, including that of low-income public housing. UDC-Greater Rochester, Inc. (UDC-GRI), a subsidiary of the state UDC, was formed, and a search was begun for improved methods that would save both time and money in the construction of high-rise apartment complexes. Three such technologies were ultimately utilized: the two industrial technologies mentioned above and a third, called the "flying form," which was nonindustrial. The flying-form method produced concrete slabs on site, using forms that could be moved from floor to floor as the building progressed.

Industrialized housing technology had no major problems at the adoption stage. UDC-GRI was backed by a strong coalition: the business community, minority groups, and the city government. The city agreed to provide the sites for twelve complexes and prepare them with the required water and sewer facilities. UDC-GRI would then buy the land and build the complexes. Financing would be provided by UDC bond issues backed by federal subsidies from the federal Department of Housing and Urban Development. Once built, the housing was expected to be self-supporting.

In implementing the program, UDC-GRI used what is referred to as a "fast-track" method that eliminated many of the formal steps usually required in conventional developments of this kind. Mainly because of fast-tracking, the newly formed firm which was to supply the components was not ready for production in time to meet the delivery requirements, and another source of supply had to be found. UDC-GRI located two established firms that would furnish the parts until the new firm was able to produce them.

Other problems in implementation were caused by design changes, panels that did not meet specifications, union requirements, and fire and safety code compliance. Changes in the European building design were necessary to conform to the American life-style; imperfect panels had to be returned or repaired on site; the union required a twenty-one-man crew on site at all times, compared to the six-man crew used in Europe; and local fire and safety codes required the installation of fire alarms which had not been included in the original specifications. All of these factors added to the time and expense of construction and defeated the original purpose of using the industrialized method of construction. The cost of constructing seven housing complexes was approximately $50 million; the estimated cost had been $31.5 million.

Upon completion of these seven complexes, UDC-GRI decided to use the newly introduced flying form technology for construction of such complexes in the future. The many problems encountered in implementing industrialized housing had defeated its incorporation in Rochester. The flying form method proved to be more cost-effective and had fewer problems in implementation. It is now used throughout the United States.

Modular Housing in Syracuse

Modular housing technology used a modular structural system designed by a Syracuse architectural engineer for the purpose of furnishing safe, low-cost, attractive apartment complexes for inner-city residents. The "module" was a box-shaped room containing built-in electrical, heating, and plumbing units. Panels for the module, made of a special concrete mixture in a structural steel frame, were welded together to form the box-shaped unit. The modules were produced in a factory and transported to the construction site where they were installed as interior rooms.

The designer and his architectural firm drew plans for a modest, mid-rise senior citizen apartment complex using the modular technology. In 1970, they approached the Syracuse Housing Authority (SHA) for adoption and funding of the project. SHA was interested and encouraging. However, before any firm commitment was made, local elections brought about a change in political power and a resulting change in SHA management and policy. SHA was no longer interested in adopting and funding modular housing technology.

In 1971, the entrepreneurs approached the New York State Urban Development Corporation (UDC). UDC confirmed the need for senior citizen housing in the proposed area of Syracuse. However, before it adopted the innovation and funded construction of the building in December 1972, HUD was assured of the approval of the mayor of Syracuse, the cooperation of SHA, which agreed to partially subsidize the project, the compliance of the city zoning board to rezone the area of the proposed site, and the approval of the residents of the neighborhood.

Two major problems arose in the adoption stage. First, UDC required extensive testing and structural analyses of the modules. Second, there was confusion over whether the electrical subcontractor had included the work of joining the modules' wiring with the building's electrical transformers and those of the utility company. In the implementation stage, there was trouble with the plumbers' union. The union insisted that the factory-installed plumbing be removed and replaced, on site, by union plumbers. These problems were costly and time consuming.

Despite the delays, construction was completed on time, and the building was dedicated by the mayor in April 1974. Although the costs were above the originally estimated $2.7 million, modular structural technology was recognized as successful. However, the technology was not utilized in Syracuse housing other than in this one building. Therefore, in reality, it has failed to become incorporated.

Many factors influenced the arrestment of the technology. The federal housing subsidy moratorium of the Nixon administration, a declining bond market, higher interest rates, and the energy crisis all prevented UDC and private companies from starting more projects that might use the system. Also, the company that manufactured the modules did not have the resources to survive, nor could it acquire them.

SOVENT Plumbing System in Syracuse

SOVENT is a plumbing vent system designed by a Swiss engineer for high-rise apartment complexes. It replaces the traditional, two-pipe vent system with a single, copper pipe system that uses special aerator and deaerator fittings for venting purposes. The advantages of SOVENT were said to be economy in material cost and ease of installation.

The New York State Urban Development Corporation (UDC) adopted SOVENT in 1970 for use in a high-rise apartment complex being funded in Syracuse. After its adoption by UDC, the use of the SOVENT system was challenged by the Onondaga County Examining Board for Plumbers and the Onondaga County Health Department. These agencies refused to approve its use on the grounds that it did not comply with county and state building construction codes on venting requirements.

UDC took the stand that as a state agency it did not need the county's approval; the county agencies maintained that SOVENT could not be used unless they approved it. This stalemate was finally resolved through the intermediary efforts of UDC's local subsidiary, the Metropolitan Development Corporation (MDC). The compromise agreed upon was that SOVENT should be subjected to performance testing as a criterion of its conformity to the state building code. This compromise was accomplished mainly because of the ability of the local head of MDC to deal effectively with both UDC and county representatives.

In Syracuse, SOVENT was implemented only in this one project. Further implementation and possible incorporation of the system did not take place because a new product, called "no-hub" casting pipe, replaced the traditional piping. No-hub pipe conformed to the local codes and was more economical to install than traditional piping because of reduced labor costs. Meanwhile, SOVENT had become more costly when the price of copper increased. Both of these factors defeated the innovative and cost-saving features of the SOVENT technology.

SOVENT was originally projected as a saving of $25,000 over traditional venting systems. The increased price of copper, competing innovation in assembling the old system, and increased labor costs caused by the novelty in SOVENT technology resulted in the final costs being $25,000 more than traditional costs.

LAW ENFORCEMENT

Coordinated Team Patrol (CTP) in Rochester

CTP is a form of team policing combining investigative and

patrol functions in the Rochester Police Department. Each of the first two experimental teams consisted of twenty-eight patrol officers, six detectives, four sergeants, and a lieutenant who was the team leader. The team's responsibility was the control of crime in its area.

CTP was instituted by the new commissioner of police on an experimental basis in 1971. It offered a possible solution to the problem of the rising crime rate. In addition, the established Criminal Investigation Division was considered by the commissioner to be inefficient, as the crime clearance rate was not keeping pace with the increase in crime.

The unique approach of CTP to criminal investigation was especially difficult to implement in the environment of the Rochester Police Department because, traditionally, there had been a separation of detective and patrol officers, with the Criminal Investigation Division having what was referred to as "its own chief." Also, there was a strong political influence that favored the detectives. Success of the CTP experimental units depended upon strong team leadership and a high degree of autonomy. In the next four years after 1971, CTP survived political changes, organizational changes, and, eventually, a change in the top leadership of the department. During this period, it received funding first from the Police Foundation and later from the Law Enforcement Assistance Administration (LEAA). The Urban Institute, under contract with the Police Foundation, provided an outside evaluation of the program, as well as help in the final plans for its incorporation city-wide.

In 1975, there was a massive reorganization of the Rochester Police Department under the leadership of the former director of planning and evaluation who had been in charge of the CTP experiment and had recently been appointed chief of police. At this time, CTP was incorporated into the department on a city-wide basis. It probably will not be easily influenced in the future by political changes since it has been structured on a merit system which mitigates possible political influence or favoritism. CTP has come to be regarded by the whole department as a very effective method for criminal investigation and crime control.

No additional police officers were hired for CTP. The costs of reorganization of the existing police force over the period of CTP introduction were subsidized by grants from the Police Foundation ($247,000) and LEAA ($117,000).

Crime Control Team (CCT) in Syracuse

CCT is a managerial innovation in which a team of police officers combines the functions of crime prevention, investigation, and control in a specified area. In the Syracuse experiment, each CCT was composed of eight police officers, with the team leader (a sergeant) responsible for the activities of the unit.

In 1968, CCT was devised and adopted by the Syracuse Police Department on an experimental basis upon the recommendation of a consultant from the Electronics Laboratory of the General Electric Company in Syracuse. He believed that this managerial innovation would be more effective than innovative hardware technology in solving the increasing problems of crime prevention, criminal investigation, and crime control in Syracuse.

Introducing CCT on an experimental basis helped to overcome departmental resistance and morale problems. Implementing it required strong leadership, intensive officer training, community support, and the cooperation of management and personnel within the department. A strong leader, who later became chief of police, was chosen to be director of the experiment. Later, as chief of police, he continued to support CCT. Special officer training requiring 240 hours was supervised mainly by General Electric personnel. Community support for the program was gained through working with the local Model Cities Neighborhood organization, funded by the federal Department of Housing and Urban Development. The last requisite, cooperation within the department, was achieved by compromises that dropped or dampened some key features of the project.

CCT has been incorporated, with more centralized control than initially planned, in seven of the twenty-three police beats in the city. The outlook for achieving the decentralization originally envisioned is uncertain, although the chief of police has indicated that he will push CCT in that direction. During 1971-72, more police officers were hired, and CCT was expanded. The costs of adoption and implementation were $1,847,000, with the federal Law Enforcement Assistance Administration funding $1,032,468. Estimated incorporation costs have been $1,125,000 annually for personnel alone. CCT represents approximately 20 percent of the Syracuse police force.

School Resource and Information Program (SRIP) in Syracuse

SRIP is a managerial innovation that uses specially trained units of plainclothes police officers in the schools to provide security and improved communications between the police department and school community.

Following a rapid rise in racially motivated school violence in the late 1960s, the mayor of Syracuse announced the adoption of SRIP on November 25, 1970. SRIP was modeled after similar programs in other communities, especially the pioneering program in Flint, Michigan. This adoption had little opposition and was supported by educators, the police department, local government, and most of the Syracuse community, all of which felt that strong action was necessary to restore order to city schools.

SRIP was implemented under the direction of the head of the Syracuse Police Department Youth Division who recruited officers on a volunteer basis that had experience in youth-oriented activities and could be expected to gain the trust of students. Implementation was accelerated in late September 1970 because of a new surge of violence in the schools which called for immediate action. Thus, implementation of the program by school and police officials may have actually begun before November when the mayor officially announced its adoption.

The success of SRIP depended both upon the police officers adapting to the complexities of the school environment and upon the school personnel and students being reassured that the presence of police officers in the schools would not result in a police-state atmosphere within the schools. In summer 1971, funds for special training of the officers involved were provided by the federal Law Enforcement Assistance Administration. By fall 1971, initial problems of the program had been generally resolved. The officers were beginning to establish strong lines of communication with all segments of the school community; and administrators, faculty, and students became more willing to call upon the officers for assistance.

Redeploying police officers to schools entailed start-up costs, primarily for training, which came both from the department ($10,000) and from LEAA ($20,000). The annual budget for this activity was $300,000 in 1977. The cost of the program is considered less than the cost of the conventional, episodic approach to school violence.

SRIP has been incorporated in the Syracuse schools. A very close, supportive relationship exists between the officers and school principals. In addition, because the program has been useful in solving crimes and preventing violence outside the school system, it is very popular with the police department and the city administration.

SOLID WASTE DISPOSAL AND RESOURCE RECOVERY

Resource Recovery in Rochester/Monroe County

Monroe County is building a new $50.5 million resource recovery plant (expected to be completed in 1981) to process municipal solid waste. This major innovation will produce a refuse-derived fuel (RDF) and recover metal and glass. Approximately 60 percent of the plant's output will be RDF, and 30 percent will be recovered glass and metal. The remaining 10 percent will be landfill. The county-owned system will be capable of handling 2000 tons of solid waste per day from the participating towns of the county and the city of Rochester. A subsidiary of Raytheon Corporation, a major aerospace and defense contractor, designed the system and is responsible for supervising the construction of the plant, which it will operate when completed. This plant will be one of the largest operations of its kind in the nation.

The solid waste disposal problem of Monroe County and the city of Rochester intensified in 1971 when many of the local landfill sites were forced to close because they did not comply with state sanitary codes and the state moved to establish and operate a landfill for Rochester's refuse in one of the suburbs. In February 1971, the county legislative majority leader, a professional engineer, persuaded the Rochester Engineering Society (RES) to undertake a major study of solid waste disposal technologies for Monroe County. In March 1971, the county legislature created the Environmental Management Council (EMC) as an official advisory group, with emphasis on solid waste management. RES and EMC formed an alliance that advocated resource recovery as the best solution to the solid waste problem; and, in February 1972, they jointly released OPERATION: RESOURCE, recommending shredding and landfilling as temporary measures to be used until resource recovery technology and markets were made available. In the next five years, the momentum of this coalition succeeded in overcoming opposition, including many alternatives to resource recovery which were advanced.

In September 1976, the Monroe County resource recovery plant was adopted and approved for bonding by the county legislature. This adoption represented the establishment of a new function for the county government: the consolidation of solid waste management in the Monroe County Department of Public Works. With $32 million coming from the county, the New York State Department of Environmental Conservation, under a 1972 Environmental Quality Bond Act, provided the additional $18.5 million needed to implement the decision to acquire resource recovery.

To make the plant's operation economically feasible, the county plans to sell the recovered metal and glass and refuse-derived fuel. The expectation is that the money from the sale of these products will defray operating expenses of the plant. Three companies have agreed to buy the recovered materials, and the Rochester Gas and Electric Company has agreed to allow the coal burning boilers in one of its energy generating plants to be converted to the use of RDF as a supplement to coal. The utility company also agreed to lease land to the county for a receiving station and to provide design and ancillary services for the station and boiler conversion. If the new fuel is satisfactory, the utility company will purchase about one-half of the RDF output for its plant. In its present form, the fuel cannot be transported easily or stored safely. Hence, if the product is to be marketed elsewhere, a process for compacting it will probably need to be developed.

The county has taken substantial risks. If the project does not unfold as expected, the county will have to take most of the responsibility, financially and politically. The economic success of the venture depends heavily upon the acceptability of the fuel supplement and the ability to improve it for shipment and storage in order to expand its market. Resource recovery in Rochester/Monroe County has thus been adopted and is being implemented. Its prospects for incorporation appear good.

Solid Waste Shredding Machines in Syracuse/Onondaga County

Solid waste shredding machines reduce the volume of municipal solid waste by grinding it into small particles. The shredded material is unattractive to flies and vermin, practically odorless, does not blow around, and extends the life of sanitary landfills. Thus, it is considered to be more acceptable in landfilling operations than untreated solid waste.

In the late 1960s, the city of Syracuse was running short of landfill sites in which to dispose of its increasing volume of solid waste. Both the city and Onondaga County had been affected by the new, rigid state regulations regarding the maintenance of landfill sites. Some sites had to be closed, and the cost of maintaining the rest in accordance with state standards was rising rapidly. In 1967, the county intervened, hiring a consulting firm to study the problem. Later, a citizens' committee was appointed by County Executive John Mulroy to recommend a solution to the problem based on the findings of the study.

The committee advocated that a county-level agency be established to handle solid waste disposal for all local jurisdictions. It also called for the use of shredding machines for treating solid waste before it was landfilled. These recommendations were accepted by the political leaders of Onondaga County and Syracuse. In 1970, at the county's request, an Onondaga County Solid Waste Disposal Authority (SWDA) was created by the state, and a search for a supplier of shredding technology was begun.

While this search was underway, the political climate in the city was changing. In 1969, a Democratic mayor and city council were elected. The former mayor had been a Republican and had worked closely with the Republican county executive and legislature. The new mayor did not wish to lose control of solid waste management to the county SWDA. He was not impressed with the shredding technology and opposed building a plant to house shredders. Instead, he preferred that the city manage solid waste disposal as it always had.

This delayed the adoption process because SWDA not only needed the city's solid waste to make the project economically feasible, but it also needed the city's financial help in bonding for the new facility. By summer 1970, it became apparent to the mayor and city council that soon all of their available landfill space would be exhausted. Also, about this time, the Monsanto Corporation became interested in SWDA's proposed shredding operations for its own experimental purposes. Monsanto was influential in assisting SWDA to obtain an award for $211,466 from the U.S. Department of Health, Education, and Welfare's (HEW) Bureau of Solid Waste.

This federal aid, together with a growing awareness of the urgency of solving the city's solid waste landfill problems, helped persuade the mayor to enter into an agreement with SWDA. According to the terms of this arrangement, formally announced September 2, 1970, the city would (1) build a plant to house two shredders; (2) finance SWDA's bonding for the plant and lease it to SWDA until the bonds were paid off; and (3) furnish SWDA all of the city's solid waste for shredding and landfilling. In return, SWDA would provide landfill sites for the city's refuse until the shredders were in operation.

Implementation of the decision proved difficult. Monsanto withdrew because the program did not fulfill its requirements.

SWDA then contracted with Eidal, the firm that had been favored by Monsanto to supply the technology. The first shredder was put into operation in 1973 and the second shredder was completed and put into operation in 1974. A third shredder, housed in a plant at a second site, has been constructed. It has been operated only to a limited extent.

Once the shredders were built, utilizing all three became a problem. SWDA had difficulty locating landfill sites despite the use of shredded solid waste. Local opposition usually erupted when SWDA announced proposed landfill locations. Although SWDA has the power to condemn land for landfill use, it has not had the political power to override intense local opposition. Further, only three towns have contracts with SWDA; the others prefer to manage their own solid waste disposal. Without sufficient solid waste to process, there is underutilization of the two operating shredders. Until SWDA has control over solid waste in the county and can fully utilize the shredders and until regional landfills have been established, implementation cannot be considered complete, and incorporation is limited.

Over a four-year period, capital investment for the three shredders housed on two sites came to $6.49 million. The breakdown is as follows: $1.4 million city bonding for the first building; a $211,466 HEW Bureau of Solid Waste grant for the first shredder; $300,000 state Department of Environmental Conservation funds for the second shredder; $880,000 local SWDA bonding with the city's contract as collateral; and $3.7 million total county bonding for the third shredder at the second building site. Operating expenses are much more difficult to determine. However, at the time of this study, the county was contributing $50,000 per month to subsidize SWDA's shredder operations.

Resource Recovery in Syracuse/Onondaga County

In 1974, Carrier Corporation, a manufacturer of air conditioning equipment, decided to enter the resource recovery field. For its initial venture, it saw the potential of converting the

Syracuse University steam station, which heats and cools about 70 buildings at the university and in downtown Syracuse, to a resource recovery operation. It approached Syracuse University regarding selling the steam station and Onondaga County on adopting the technology. Syracuse University and the county agreed to conduct a feasibility study. The results of the study indicated that Carrier should proceed with a proposal.

Utilizing its engineering expertise and the experiences of similar projects in Europe and in Nashville, Tennessee, Carrier designed a water-wall incineration system that would burn shredded solid waste from the two operating county Solid Waste Disposal Authority shredder plants to generate steam in the Syracuse University steam station. Shredded waste would be transferred to the resource recovery plant by truck or rail. Cranes would transfer the waste from the storage pit to a hopper from which the refuse would drop onto a gate. There, it would be mixed with air and be burned as it travelled through the combustion chamber. The generated heat would produce steam which would then be transported through an existing underground distribution system to a plant for production of chilled water (to be used in air conditioning) and to the Syracuse University and Onondaga County buildings for heating purposes. In January 1976, Carrier's proposal was completed and presented to the county legislature.

To construct the plant at the estimated cost of $48.5 million, the county would need outside funding. The New York State Department of Environmental Conservation (DEC) allocated $14.6 million for the project, but this funding depended upon, among other considerations, the ability of the project to meet strict DEC requirements regarding environmental soundness, the priority of this project over others in the state, and the degree of resource recovery. In addition, state aid would be contingent on the county's ability to guarantee sufficient solid waste to operate the plant. In addition to funding difficulties, the innovation had problems with city zoning reclassification. Neighborhood residents objected to the traffic and potential pollution caused by using the steam station as the site for the project. The proposed location is in a densely populated, low-income section of the city.

Thus, the two major issues affecting adoption were (1) county guarantee of an adequate waste stream, which depended upon voluntary commitments from the city and surrounding towns and (2) site location. As the county did not have sufficient commitments of waste to fuel the station, it bargained for support of the towns at the price of alienating the city, and, at the time of the final vote by the legislature, it had tentative commitments for 80 percent of the solid waste needed. After thus alienating the city, the county compromised by granting the city near equality as an adopter, through veto power over the site location. This subjected the adoption to a much wider sphere of decision makers, and as a result a floodgate of concern about the merits and environmental impact of the proposed project was opened. There was strong opposition from the residents in the vicinity of the steam station as well as those near a substitute site that had been suggested.

Exacerbating these problems were the strict time limitations imposed by Carrier's technical design schedule. None of the underlying issues had been resolved when construction bids were in hand, forcing the county to seek an extension from the low bidder, Grumman Ecosystems. Later, on May 3, 1977, the county legislature voted to cancel the conditional contract with Grumman, thus effectively killing the proposal for the time. Shortly thereafter, Carrier Corporation arrested its resource recovery efforts.

To date there is still no consensus among the county, the towns, and the city on the adoption of the proposal. However, a report on a recent study of the proposal, submitted to the county legislature in August 1978, stated that the Syracuse University steam station would be the only feasible location for a resource recovery plant if the technology were adopted.

TRANSPORTATION

Dial-A-Bus in Rochester/Monroe County

The dial-a-bus system in Rochester/Monroe County is a

surburban supplement to the established, fixed route, city-county bus system. A sophisticated, computer-assisted routing technology is used in this system. Small buses pick up passengers at the point of their call and carry them to a destination anywhere in the dial-a-bus area. The bus in closest proximity to the call point when the call is received responds to that call. The service originally included several plans: (1) standard service (call point to destination), (2) home to school, (3) home to work, and (4) call point to fixed-route bus stops of the Regional Transit Service (RTS). Later in the program, special buses were introduced for the elderly and handicapped clientele.

In 1969, the Rochester-Genesee Regional Transportation Authority (RTA) was created by the state to develop a master plan for transportation within its jurisdiction. One of its first moves was to take over the city-owned bus company, which it renamed the Regional Transit Service, and attempt to revitalize it. The director of RTA saw a need for an auxiliary bus system in the suburbs to supplement the established, fixed-route system and advocated the adoption of dial-a-bus. Failing to obtain federal funds for a dial-a-bus demonstration, RTA purchased a small bus company in Batavia, New York, in 1971 and conducted its own demonstration which was successful and eventually replaced the fixed-route system in that town. The following year, RTA introduced a dial-a-bus system in the Rochester suburb of Greece. To implement this system, seven twenty-five-passenger buses were purchased at a cost of $30,000 each. This was RTA's first effort in a long-range plan for a dial-a-bus network that would serve eight to ten suburban zones in the future.

At the end of its first year of operation, the dial-a-bus system in Greece, unlike that in Batavia, had a deficit of $500,000, a fact that disturbed the county legislators who had been assured by the director of RTA that it would be self-supporting. In the following year, when the county was mandated by the New York State Department of Transportation to furnish $912,000 in matching funds for dial-a-bus, the county-RTA relationship deteriorated. The director of RTA realized that if the dial-a-bus project were to survive he would have to obtain federal funds.

This time RTA's proposal to the federal Urban Mass Transportation Administration (UMTA) to fund a dial-a-bus demonstration project in the suburbs of Greece and Irondequoit met with success. UMTA provided $2,598,200 for a two-year demonstration of dial-a-bus in those two suburbs and the adjacent areas of Rochester. It also provided an additional $786,000 in capital funds. UMTA was interested in demonstrating the computer-assisted routing technology developed by the Massachusetts Institute of Technology (MIT) as well as in experimenting with several types and makes of small buses. The grant also stipulated integration of dial-a-bus with fixed-route systems as a central goal. These three requirements caused problems, however, in the implementation stage.

Soon after computer-assisted routing was in operation, the main computer facility to which the Rochester computer was linked, First Data of Waltham, Massachusetts, had a fire which resulted in a six-month shutdown. Then, when its operation was restored, there were continous tie-ups in service because of technical problems. In fact, RTA later blamed much of the trouble which prevented smooth operation of the system upon the computer-assisted technology. In addition to computer problems, RTA had difficulty servicing and repairing the fleet of small buses. First, the dial-a-bus gasoline engines were unfamiliar to the maintenance crews who were used to working on the diesel powered engines of the large city buses. Second, standardization of parts and maintenance was impossible because there were so many types and makes of the small buses. The third UMTA requirement, integration of dial-a-bus with fixed routes, did not work out. A complexity of services and fares, constantly in a state of flux, confused the public and caused the system to be undependable.

Problems in management developed because the project manager, an MIT consultant, lived in Cambridge, Massachusetts, far from the demonstration site. This meant that he was not around to attend to the day-to-day operations of the system. In addition, his main interest was in UMTA's objective, the potential of dial-a-bus for urban mass transportation on a national basis, rather than in RTA's interest in finding out whether dial-a-bus could work in the specific

Rochester area. Also, during the demonstration period, there were many changes in the top management and some of the key personnel of RTA. These changes badly weakened the organizational structure, and the whole operation suffered. All of these problems and difficulties adversely affected the successful implementation of the dial-a-bus system during the two-year demonstration period.

In June 1977, when the demonstration officially ended, RTA sought and obtained an extension of its grant from UMTA to continue the project. It was hoped that this extension would allow the system to be reevaluated and necessary adjustments to be made to steer dial-a-bus toward incorporation. It had been successful in many ways, especially late in the demonstration period, in providing a much-needed service to the elderly and handicapped. If the managerial problems could be solved, undoubtedly the technical problems would be overcome. With UMTA's continued interest and support, dial-a-bus still has a chance of becoming incorporated in Rochester and Monroe County. However, it is doubtful whether the ultimate system that would reach routinization would be as technically innovative as that originally proposed.

Dial-A-Bus in Syracuse/Onondaga County

Dial-a-bus is a demand-responsive transit system in Syracuse/Onondaga County that provides home-to-destination transportation for elderly and handicapped persons at a reduced fare. Reservations for service must be made two days in advance. The system is served by a fleet of four specially designed minibuses with seats for eight passengers and room for two wheelchairs. These buses are equipped with features such as low steps, extended guard rails, safety stanchions, special seats, and wheelchair devices designed to accommodate the physical limitations of the clientele.

In 1970, the Central New York Regional Transportation Authority (RTA) was created by New York State to deal with the increasingly complex transportation problems of the seven-county central New York area, with Syracuse as its hub. In 1972, when the Syracuse Transit Corporation that operated the city bus system was on the verge of failure, it was taken over by RTA. At about the same time, the Metropolitan Commission on Aging (MCOA), established as a joint function of the city and county, was searching for a solution to the mobility problems of the elderly.

RTA believed that a unique dial-a-bus system, designed to furnish transportation to the elderly, might provide MCOA with such a solution. Thus, working together, MCOA and RTA adopted dial-a-bus in 1972 and, with $35,000 provided by MCOA, conducted a small, one-year demonstration using one regular city bus. Shortly thereafter, RTA and MCOA established a dial-a-bus project advisory committee to study the special transportation problems of elderly people and to recommend possible solutions. Later, these recommendations formed the basis for the specifications of the special buses designed for elderly and handicapped persons.

By 1973, with a successful initial demonstration and with the cooperation of MCOA, the advisory committee, and other affected citizens' groups such as those representing handicapped persons with transportation problems, RTA had the support needed to interest the federal Urban Mass Transportation Administration (UMTA) in funding an enlarged dial-a-bus project in Syracuse and Onondaga County. In May 1973, UMTA approved RTA's proposal for a two-year dial-a-bus service demonstration for the elderly and handicapped using regular buses. In July of the same year, UMTA made an additional grant on a second proposal to acquire four specially equipped buses, which had been advocated by the advisory committee, to be used in the two-year demonstration project that would run from October 1973 to October 1975.

Funding for the two-year project totaled $500,000: UMTA, $333,000; New York State Department of Transportation (DOT), $125,000; RTA and local sources, $42,000. The special buses, designed and manufactured by Mercedes-Benz, were supplied by Keeler Motor Car Company at a cost of $200,000. This cost was funded by a grant of $133,000 from UMTA, with the remainder coming from the state DOT and local sources. By receiving the two federal grants, Syracuse was recognized as "the leading exponent in the nation offering special transportation services to the elderly and handicapped," according to the head of RTA.

To avoid being considered unfair competition to private companies and organizations that provided similar service at a much higher rate, dial-a-bus was limited to curbside service. At the end of the first year of implementation, a demand evaluation study of the project was made by RTA. This study found dial-a-bus to be most economically viable for short trips in high-demand areas. On the basis of this report, dial-a-bus service was changed from daily to weekly in the county sectors in October 1974; but the short-haul, high-demand area of the city continued to receive daily service. The demand for dial-a-bus service grew rapidly. Soon the two-day advance reservation was not sufficient, and passengers were forced to wait a longer period for rides.

When UMTA's grants expired in October 1975, dial-a-bus was incorporated by RTA. It had been very successful. Under the federal Urban Mass Transportation Act of 1975, dial-a-bus was able to receive federal operating funds, but only in the amount that was matched locally. The demand for dial-a-bus service is now greater than RTA can supply. If service is to expand, local funding must be increased in order to obtain more federal funds to support the additional cost.

OTHER INNOVATIONS IN SYRACUSE/ ONONDAGA COUNTY

Computerized Assessment in the Town of Manlius, Onondaga County

The real property tax administration of the town of Manlius, a suburb of Syracuse, uses a computer system as an analytical tool in the preparation of appraisals. The computer tests variables relating to the value of property and the neighborhood and applies them to the appraisal of individual properties with similar characteristics to produce an estimate of value. Utilization of this technology requires specialized, skilled personnel.

In 1970, the state legislature passed an assessment improvement bill that required legislative bodies at the local level to appoint a full-time assessor for a six-year term and to establish a board of assessment review. The bill also created the post of county director of real property tax services through which counties were to provide assessment services to municipalities. The changes flowing from this bill fed back into the state administrative level to produce many managerial innovations, one of which was the use of the computer in the preparation of appraisals.

In the first half of 1971, the assessment procedures in Manlius were not only affected by the state bill that was going into effect in September, but also by a taxpayers' revolt in which many of the citizens organized to protest the increasing inequity of tax assessments in the town. Town officials, sensing the time propitious for change, held a town meeting in September to discuss the assessment problem. The results of this meeting were (1) to effect a town-wide reappraisal program, and (2) to call for the replacement of the existing board of assessors with a well-qualified, single assessor and staff. They would hold regular conferences with the town board, as well as obtain all possible assistance from the Onondaga County Department of Finance and the state Board of Equalization and Assessment. The reappraisal program was to be conducted within budgetary limitations and completed as soon as possible.

On October 1, 1971, the incumbent assessor and former chairman of the board of assessors was appointed to the six-year term of office provided for by the new state law. The citizens' group objected to this person's reappointment because of his perceived failure to equitably appraise town property during the twelve years he had held office. The upcoming November election stimulated town officials to respond to this criticism, and, in late October, they appointed a knowledgeable local appraiser and real estate broker to the assessor's staff. In January 1972, the assessor resigned, and the appraiser was appointed to fill his unexpired term of office.

Shortly after taking office, the new assessor attended the New York State Assessors' Association Conference where he met the director of local assessment services and the director of data processing of the state board. Through this contact, the state board became interested in having Manlius serve as one of three test areas in which mass appraisal techniques would be applied in a computer model to the continuous annual revaluation of a town's tax base. The assessor returned with the proposal that the town consider being included in the state program which he saw as a means of efficiently fulfilling the obligations of his office to revalue the town tax base in a professionally acceptable manner at a minimal cost.

In April 1972, the Manlius town officials met in Albany with state board officials to discuss a formal program. Following this meeting, there was a two-year period of evaluation during which the program was developed by the state and local assessor's office, and town officials were educated concerning the process and its impact on local assessments. In this evaluation period, the state provided expert personnel, computer time, and programs; the town allotted existing personnel and agreed to purchase printouts and pay for the keypunching of the data.

In 1974, to ensure successful implementation of the program, there was an active public relations effort to explain each step of the reappraisal process to the taxpayers. The local newspaper ran a series of informative articles. In February and March, the state board and town officials held a series of public information meetings that were considered very successful. In May, impact notices and notices of comparable valuations were sent to all property owners, estimating the tax on their property. The assessor's office willingly answered any questions concerning the assessments. Although a small group started law suits over their assessments, none were pursued to trial, and computerized assessment proceeded to be implemented.

The state experimental implementation ended in August 1976. During the period 1973-1976, the town had spent $93,000. After state withdrawal, incorporation costs would approximate an additional $30,000 a year if Manlius hired a private service company to supply the technology, or an additional $15,000 a year if it used county services. Subsequently, the town took over the program and subcontracted with Onondaga County for computer services.

In summer 1978, following the conclusion of our research, a new taxpayers' revolt started in opposition to the computerized assessment program on the grounds that it, too, caused inequity in the treatment of individual properties. This matter is still ongoing at the time of this writing.

Cable Television (CATV) in Syracuse

Cable Television (CATV) is not a new technology. It has been commercially available for over twenty years. In a typical system, large, central antennas receive over-the-air signals from distant stations which are then amplified, processed, and transmitted over a network of coaxial cables. The average cable system provides 25 to 35 channels and possesses the capability of two-way communication. However, it is possible to install more complicated terminals such as tape recorders, two-way voice and picture communication devices, printout machines, and alarm systems for fire protection and law enforcement purposes.

Under Federal Communications Commission (FCC) regulations, adoption of CATV was prohibited in the 100 largest urban markets, which included Syracuse, until 1972. As soon as it was permitted, Syracuse began a research and planning program to obtain a municipal franchise for a CATV system under the procedures established by FCC and the New York State Cable Commission. The mayor appointed an advisory committee on cable television which proceeded to engage the services of a local consulting firm with expertise in electronics. This committee provided the Syracuse Common Council with a report containing a general discussion of CATV (technical information, economic analysis, and financial forecast) and a discussion of ownership alternatives: municipal, private company, and not-for-profit company. The committee recommended municipal ownership because it believed that the potential of the technology could be better realized under a municipal system and that revenues from the system would be substantial.

The common council appointed a cable television committee which decided to implement the recommendation of the mayor's advisory committee that a municipally-owned cable system be established. However, restrictions in state law regarding municipal bonding for a CATV system eventually proved to be an insurmountable barrier to municipal ownership of the system. In June 1975, Syracuse made an unsuccessful effort to obtain a change in the law.

Then, in 1976, attention was directed to the possibility that the city could bond for a portion of the system. A municipal sensor monitoring system that could provide fire, burglar, and medical alarms was proposed and received the active support of many people, including the fire chief. In their search for a supplier of the technology, the common council wanted assurance that these services, as well as a municipal access channel for local programming, would be provided by the privately-owned company.

During the long search period, the members of the common council had been under constant pressure from advocates of CATV who were interested only in its entertainment features and who complained over the long delay caused by the inclusion of these special features in the proposed system. Nevertheless, the council was adamant, and the president named a specifications review committee to establish parameters of the system for which bids would be accepted. In June 1976, the committee presented a plan to the council for an $18.5 million municipal sensor cable monitoring system.

The city sent out requests for proposals that would conform to its specifications; and, in August 1977, Canadian Cablesystems, Ltd., of Toronto was selected. Canadian Cablesystems, Ltd., and a group of local investors then formed a partnership and established a new company, Syracuse Cablesystems, to build and operate the system. In addition to providing twelve channels and Home Box Office for entertainment, Syracuse Cablesystems would test an alarm system in one thousand homes, provide an access channel for programs of local origin, and invest $680,000 in equipment to televise the programs. Although the system installed by Syracuse Cablesystems will be privately-owned, it will be subject to state regulations as well as terms of contracts negotiated with the city of Syracuse periodically.

On August 23, 1978, the New York State Commission on Cable Television unanimously approved the Syracuse Cablesystems application to build and operate a cable system in Syracuse. Syracuse Cablesystems does not expect any problem in obtaining the approval of FCC; and, barring unexpected delays such as that caused by exceptionally severe winter weather, CATV should reach the first customers by early spring 1979.

The decision-making process and technical problems have been time-consuming; but, once the system is in operation, the city of Syracuse will have one of the most innovative CATV systems in North America.

4
Technological Choice

This study focuses on organizational and political issues related to technological innovation in urban public services. In each case, the issues revolve around the decision-making process behind the choices. However, it is essential to emphasize the range of technologies about which local governments make decisions. Before positing the basic questions of *who, how,* and *why* in decision making, it is first necessary to ask the question: *What* is the nature of the technology being introduced or rejected? Are the technologies neutral, or do they make a difference in the decision-making outcomes? In looking at the influence of various individuals and groups on the decision-making process, there is a tendency to neglect the possible effects of the innovation itself. This is a mistake. The evidence in our research suggests that all technologies are not created equal; some are easier to adopt and implement than others. If the mini-pumper had been a maxi-pumper, would the process have worked differently? Had the shredder been a composter or an incinerator, how would the Syracuse solid waste disposal case have read?

Technologies vary greatly. It is difficult, in fact, to arrive at a generally accepted, operationally useful definition of technology, to say nothing of establishing areas of congruence among the innovations we have been studying.[30] In the literature on technology and society, some writers have chosen to take a broad view, treating technology as any tool or method that man uses to accomplish his goals. At the other end of the spectrum are those who take a much more restrictive view of technology and regard it essentially as hardware—devices invented on the basis of scientific knowledge and applied to practical purposes.

In this study, we have chosen to consider technology as something more than hardware. The innovations we have studied include software systems such as the Crime Control Team (CCT) in Syracuse and the similar Coordinated Team Patrol (CTP) in Rochester in which hardware plays a relatively minor role. On the other hand, several consist of hardware devices with complex engineering aspects such as the solid waste shredder in Syracuse and the resource recovery systems in Rochester and Syracuse. There are also mixed software-hardware systems such as the mini-pumper and the educational innovations in both cities in which hardware is an important element but is inextricably embedded in a much broader innovative context.

Technology does make a difference, but how much difference it makes is exceedingly difficult to judge. There are so many variables at work simultaneously. Ideally, in order to factor out the technological variables, we would have to control: (1) the overall functional setting, (2) the nature of the particular governmental unit concerned, and (3) the type of strategy employed by the entrepreneur, while varying the nature of the technological innovation. This is, of course, an impossible set of conditions, so we must be satisfied with a qualitative analysis in which we look as systematically as possible for similarities and differences among the technologies, attempt to understand them in their contexts, and isolate causes and effects, or at least associated events, through patterns in the data.

Characterizing the Technologies

The first step in our analysis is to characterize the technologies involved in the cases. A basic assumption is that we are primarily concerned with exogenous rather than endogenous characteristics of the technologies. That is, we are not interested in the technical aspects of the innovations for their own sake, but only insofar as these aspects affect factors such as cost, performance, perceptions of decision makers, and the range of actors involved. Bearing this in mind, we can identify several attributes that appear relevant to understanding the ways in which technology operates as a variable. These attributes are: (1) degree of change the technologies require in existing operating patterns; (2) cost; (3) reversibility; (4) separability (i.e., susceptibility to trial implementation); (5) complexity and sophistication; (6) operability/feasibility; and (7) range of impact. This chapter discusses the nature and significance of these attributes and points out where they were important to the outcome of the particular innovations studied. These attributes, it should be noted, are not "pure." They are interrelated and overlap each other. Subsequent analysis may perhaps permit isolation of a smaller number of basic attributes.

Degree of Change

A key aspect of the innovation is the degree of change in current operating patterns that it requires. One would expect incremental innovations to be easier to adopt and implement than radical ones. Drawing the line between them, however, may prove to be a difficult judgmental issue in practice. What seems to count is the incrementalism of the innovation as perceived by those who have a stake in the decision-making process. Some innovations such as resource recovery and team policing are clearly not incremental; but, if no incremental alternatives are available, the adopters and implementers may not object to the radicalism of the innovation. However, this was not the case in the Syracuse Campus Plan and SOVENT. Both required radical change, and both had detractors because of the availability of less radical alternatives. On the other hand, the mini-pumper in Rochester overcame firefighter opposition because its introduction was purposely kept on a strictly incremental basis.

Cost

Cost is crucial in affecting the acceptability of an innovation. We may hypothesize that expensive technologies are more difficult to adopt than cheap ones. The cost issue is not entirely straightforward, however. The cost of an innovation must be gauged relative to the share of the governmental budget allocated to the relevant functional area. Just as it is relatively easier to spend $10 million for defense in the federal budget than it is to spend a similar amount for environmental protection, cost expectations also vary among urban functions. Thus, functional areas that have traditionally received little funding tend to be more cost-sensitive than those known to be expensive.

In general, the cost of an innovation influences the range of actors who must participate in the decision process, as well as the public visibility of that process. *Ceteris paribus*, the costlier an innovation, the lengthier and more controversial is the decision-making process. A critical aspect of the cost issue is whether the innovation can be bought with existing departmental funds or whether a special expenditure from capital funds is required. Technological innovations that fall into the latter category, particularly where large-scale bonding is necessary, are truly major decisions and involve the whole range of governmental decision-making mechanisms. An excellent example of this distinction can be found in the contrast between the fire reporting system, UFIRS, and resource recovery. UFIRS cost only about $2500, and its acquisition barely made a ripple in Syracuse. However, resource recovery in both Syracuse and Rochester involved decisions to spend more than had ever been spent with local funds. The subsequent scrutiny of these proposed expenditures meant that reaching a decision took years, rather than weeks or months.

Another aspect of the cost issue relates to the operating expenses of proposed innovations. For some innovations, the operating costs dwarf the immediate costs of acquisition. This issue has proven especially critical in the Syracuse and Rochester dial-a-bus cases. Cost in these cases was not an issue initially, but mounting operating deficits later drew criticism from local officials who were responsible for the debts.

The issue of cost, of course, can be sidestepped if local adopters are able to obtain outside funds. Thus, the housing innovations and dial-a-bus in both cities, the Crime Control Team, and Project Unique never would have been undertaken if local funds were the only source of support, but the availability of federal funds reduced the salience of the cost issue in these cases.

Reversibility

Generally, the cost of an innovation affects its reversibility. The more an innovation costs to implement, the more difficult it is likely to be to discard the innovation and try something else, even if the results of the innovation are not satisfactory. Reversibility also depends on whether the technology replaces a former means of performing some function and whether, by its nature, it destroys that formers means. In such cases, even if the new technology does not perform as well as expected, those who are supposed to be served by it will not abandon it, for if they did, they could be worse off than they were previously. The conceptual distinction between implementation and incorporation essentially disappears in such cases. Once the innovation has been implemented, it must be incorporated. There is no turning back from such decisions. When decision makers recognize this, the adoption decision becomes more difficult. This occurred in the adoption of the mini-pumper in Syracuse. The city council was being asked to approve bonds for a large expenditure that would have the effect of completely revamping firefighting operations in Syracuse. The council was reluctant to move quickly on such an important, irreversible decision, and the fire chief was forced to devise strategies to hasten the decision-making process.

Separability

The essence of this factor is the extent to which the technology lends itself to partial implementation on a trial basis. In the case of some technological innovations, constructing a prototype or perhaps implementing only part of a planned innovation can serve as a means of reducing the risk and avoiding the possibility of catastrophic failure in full-scale implementation. Other technologies, termed "nonseparable," do not lend themselves to such a step-wise process. One might expect their implementation to prove more difficult on this account. Nonseparable technological innovations that are also expensive and hard to reverse would seem to pose particular difficulties.

The separability issue was especially prominent in the education cases in Syracuse and Rochester. Both Campus Plan and Project Unique had similar objectives of reducing de facto segregation and generally improving the quality of elementary instruction. These objectives were controversial, and programs to promote them were bound to encounter difficulties in adoption and implementation.

The success of Project Unique and the failure of Campus Plan are largely attributable to the design of the programs. In Rochester, the program was separated into a number of components. Some proved more controversial or less effective than others and were eliminated along the way. But key components survived, leaving the Rochester School District with something to show for its efforts. In Syracuse, however, the program was submitted as a take-it-or-leave-it, unitary package, highly visible and easily open to attack. Despite the merits of various aspects of the program, the entire innovation was rejected.

In other cases, trial implementations were possible and contributed to the complete adoption of an innovation. Such demonstrations occurred in OPTICOM, CCT, and dial-a-bus in both cities.

Complexity and Sophistication

A technological innovation that is complex and sophisticated is also likely to be expensive. But complexity and sophistication mean more than expense. They also require specialized expertise to install, service, and, in some cases, operate the technology. Such expertise may or may not be readily available to the government agency involved. Often the agency must acquire it from outside, thereby placing itself at the mercy or convenience of external organizations which may have different sets of priorities and which may sometimes introduce delays or service interruptions.

The more complex and sophisticated a technology is, the more prone it usually is to breakdowns, unless it is very carefully handled and properly maintained. In some cases, too, it may be more difficult for decision makers to understand the important aspects and recognize the benefits of the technology.

Complex and sophisticated technologies may be prestigious additions to operations of city government. Political leaders can point to them with pride, as evidence of the sophistication and progressivism of their administrations. When they do not perform in the expected manner, however, such innovations can backfire on their sponsors and become highly visible symbols of waste and mismanagement—expensive technological white elephants.

Probably the clearest example of the detrimental influence of this attribute is the case of the solid waste shredders in Syracuse. At the time of adoption, shredder technology was in its infancy. Few engineers had a good understanding of the shredders that were adopted. Indeed, this was a primary reason for its adoption, as a federal grant was available to test innovative shredders. During implementation, maintenance proved much more of a problem than expected. In fact, the cost of keeping the shredders in service is a primary reason why the future of solid waste shredding in Onondaga County is uncertain.

The complexity of resource recovery also proved to be an almost intractable problem in Onondaga and Monroe Counties. Few engineers, much less local legislators, understood the operation of the proposed resource recovery plants. As a result, legislators were more prone to approve funding for further design studies than for the projects themselves.

Another example is the Rochester dial-a-bus, which employed much more complex technology than did its counterpart in Syracuse. Political officials in Rochester allowed the technology to overshadow the importance of service delivery to users. When service suffered, the complexity of the innovation was easily targeted for special blame. Adopters will not defend what they do not understand.

On rare occasions, complexity can work to an innovation's benefit. Organized criticism of the computerized assessment program was very difficult to sustain, since most taxpayers did not understand its operation. Also, in the Rochester mini-pumper case, when firefighters appealed to the public in their struggle against implementation of the innovation, the arguments were so complex that the public put its trust in the established experts, the fire department leadership. However, these two cases may be quite unusual. Very rarely is the burden of proof put on the detractors of an urban service.

Operability/Feasibility

Technological innovations vary in their novelty, from concepts that have never before been operationally tested to items that are already in use in many other cities and are new only in the present context. The degree to which the feasibility of a technological innovation has been operationally tested is a key characteristic for our purposes. The more hardware-centered a technology is, the easier it is for decision makers to assess its performance on the basis of experience in other settings. If a technological device can be purchased with given specifications at a given cost and if sufficient data on its past performance are available, risk is reduced, and adoption and implementation are simplified. If the technological innovation is managerial or otherwise software-centered, then its feasibility in different settings is less easy to evaluate, and each implementation is considered more or less unique. Proven feasibility is less important in separable technologies, those that lend themselves to partial implementation or demonstration, as well as those that are easily reversible.

The operability of the innovation was important in several cases. It is unlikely that Rapid Water and OPTICOM would have been adopted by the Syracuse Fire Department had it not been for recent, favorable experience with them in other cities. In both resource recovery cases, failures in other cities were cited by opponents of the innovation, increasing the difficulty of adoption. When innovations have not been previously proven, extraordinary circumstances are required to win over local adopters. Modular and industrial housing and SOVENT, for example, were practically unknown in this country. The massive commitment of the New York State Urban Development Corporation was required to stimulate local adoption.

Impact

Some technologies have perceptible impacts on broad segments of the population. Others are of interest and concern only to a limited group. Impact is associated with visibility and with the range of actors involved in the decision-making process. To some extent, impact is a function of the area in which the innovation is applied. Thus, any innovation involving education is bound to receive the close scrutiny of parents, as was the case with Campus Plan and Project Unique. Other high-visibility functions are transportation, housing, and police. At the opposite end of the spectrum are fire and solid waste disposal. Few citizens are directly aware of the quality of delivery of these services. Therefore, innovations in these areas generally do not attract much attention, except, for example, in cases where questions of siting of firehouses and resource recovery plants arise.

Within a given functional area, however, certain innovations may relate more closely than others to deep-seated values. Other things being equal, these innovations are likely to be more disputatious than others. It is here that attributes of the innovation can be related most concretely to decision making. If we know the adopters and implementers and can judge the nature and intensity of their stakes in a given innovation, we can probably predict the relative ease or difficulty in the adoption and use of the technology. For example, all existing organizations have technical cores, in the sense of a dominant activity closest to the mission of the organization. Those who perform this activity constitute a dominant elite within the organization. Technologies that threaten this technical core will be difficult to incorporate in an organization.

Thus, team policing in both Rochester and Syracuse threatened various groups in the police departments, especially detectives, and overcoming such opposition was a major struggle. To a lesser extent, this was also true in the adoption of Rapid Water in Syracuse and the mini-pumper in Rochester. Law enforcement and fire protection are old established functions, and new approaches almost invariably threaten someone in these organizations. Knowledge of the potential impact in advance of adoption can prepare the way for a smooth incorporation.

Some technologies augment the role of an existing activity within the organization, and in society generally. The organization will wish to adopt and use these technologies. The point, therefore, is that organizations do not fear innovations per se; they fear innovations that oppose the interest of dominant elites within them. They like innovations that improve their relative ability to perform their existing activity and to expand that activity within the larger setting.

However, what is good for the organization may not be good for groups in the community external to it. Deeper change, altering the technical core and the fundamental way the organization carries out its task, may be what some groups believe is needed in terms of innovation. Such groups tend to be outside the organization, however, for their views are invariably seen as a threat rather than an aid to the entity that is the focus of their efforts.

Conclusion

We have discussed a number of attributes of innovation that are significant to technological choice in local government, and, in doing so, we have come full circle. Technologies do vary in terms of incrementalism/racialism in an objective sense. Some are genuinely new to the world, such as atomic energy and space technology. But most innovations are incremental or radical only in terms of the potential user. Consider, for example, the introduction of cable TV to Syracuse. Cable TV was new to that city, but not to other cities. However, it was so new to Syracuse that it constituted a new function or urban service, and as a consequence, its introduction became a major political controversy.

What are the perceived impacts of the innovation on the user? Are they favorable or unfavorable? How much do they help or hurt? Whom do they favor or hinder? What groups outside the user organization regard them as affecting their stakes? Technology cannot be disembodied from institutions with which it is, or is intended to be, aligned. A technology is viewed through the eyes of existing groups and organizations. What happens to a technology, particularly in respect to decisions to adopt and use, depends not on its inherent beauty but on how it looks to certain beholders.

5
Placing Innovations on the Agenda

Who makes technological choices in local government? Why? How? Why is one innovation chosen rather than another innovation or a noninnovative technology? From what sources and how are funds for innovation derived? As the previous chapter indicates, the answers to these and other questions depend considerably on the nature of the technology sought for acquisition. Its characteristics greatly affect the entire decision-making process. However, these technologies are introduced through choices made by humans and their institutions. There is no technological determinism at work. There is, instead, a decision-making process involving the interaction between technology and local governmental institutions. Thus, the nature of this interaction, seen from the vantage point of local government, is at issue here.

The character of the interaction and the strategies of those who are involved determine the course of technological change at the local level. A successfully incorporated innovation reveals an institutional structure, a bureaucracy-centered coalition. The innovation is used by a public organization that wants it. The bureaucracy is surrounded by a support system of interests that also exerts pressure for the retention of the innovation. The necessary actors—adopters, implementers, clients, and suppliers—have a stable relationship. They constitute what is, in effect, a standing alliance and system of support for the innovation. What is necessary to get to this point in the innovation process? Who takes the innovation this far? These are the questions for which we seek answers in this and the succeeding three chapters. Answers are needed to understand the process of local government innovation and the pressures that determine the course and pace of that process.

In the preadoption phase, the problem is to get an innovation on the local decision-making agenda. This means that someone in authority in local government must desire the innovation, or at least want it considered seriously for adoption. Under most circumstances, this entails gaining the commitment of a line agency. The critical linkage is between the entrepreneur and the management of the organization. A local agency's commitment does not imply adoption by local government per se. It does suggest the commitment of a potential adopter. The linkage also provides the entrepreneur an institutional base in government from which to advocate.

Awareness

The literature on innovation and change is clear about one point. Complacent people and organizations do not innovate. Nothing happens unless there is a sense of "performance gap,"[31] which means that a public service is not being delivered as well as it might be. For some reason, there are problems in the effectiveness or efficiency of service delivery. The problem may be frustration because the particular entity charged with delivery does not have all the equipment and managerial techniques that it could have to do the optimum job.

What is the nature of this performance gap? Who feels it? What difference does it make? Performance gap is subjective in many ways. A certain amount of perceived performance gap is inevitable and, insofar as preventing complacence, desirable. However, there are performance gaps of a more objective kind that are certainly undesirable, such as a rising crime rate, deteriorating housing, falling educational scores of students, and mass transit systems that are losing ridership.

The difficulty in relating such performance gaps to innovation is that they are hardly new in an urban setting. They are even recognized by those decision makers closest to the service delivery problems, the administrators of the line agencies. Administrators in local government know that they have problems in delivering services. They are aware that their agency's performance is not as effective or efficient as it could be. They usually have been among the first to view with alarm deteriorating schools, inadequate space for solid waste disposal, or inadequate transit service for the elderly and handicapped. The issue, therefore, is not awareness of problems or opportunities or the dilemma of performance gaps; the issue is how and under what conditions action for dealing with these performance gaps can take place. The answer lies in two ingredients: the existence of an entrepreneur within local government, and the existence of a trigger external to local government that serves to activate urban decision making and smooth the way for the local entrepreneur.

Entrepreneurship

Entrepreneur is a role that different individuals or groups can fill at varying phases of an innovation's decision-making process. Entrepreneurship during preadoption and adoption typically shifts to a different person during implementation. All entrepreneurs, however, serve the function of linking not only problem with solution, but technology with the political support systems necessary to make innovation possible. They link the processes of adoption with those of implementation and incorporation, and as the dynamic element within the city, obtain decisions favorable to innovation. Entrepreneurs are a pressure for change.

Two kinds of capacities are necessary in entrepreneurs: one is a technical or professional capacity to match problem with solution; the other is a political capacity to build a coalition of support around the innovation in an urban context. The two types of abilities are not necessarily complementary in the same individual. There are occasions when the technical abilities of entrepreneurs get in the way of their political skills. All entrepreneurs have to play the role of advocate, but some go beyond advocacy to zealotry. The zealous entrepreneur is an individual whose behavior is stimulated primarily by technical certainty often growing out of an inner sense of direction or vision. Zealots possess an arrogance that seems to imply, "I am

right; you are wrong; and I will move ahead in spite of you!" In
the words of lay philosopher Eric Hoffer, an entrepreneur is a
"true believer." In the literature of innovation, entrepreneurs
often emerge as product champions who will go to extraordinary lengths to achieve their purpose. An example of a
successful zealot in a governmental arena is Hyman Rickover
in the Navy. Unsuccessful zealots are legion. Because they fail
to achieve their purposes, we seldom hear about them. They
become expendable entrepreneurs.

The successful advocate-entrepreneurs are more other-
directed. They take account of the forces in their environment
in order to move toward their goals. They zig and zag, often
taking half a loaf, or whatever they can get. Such entrepreneurs
are usually better politicians than zealots because they are
willing to adapt and find areas of compromise.

The two styles can be seen in many walks of life. As zealots
differ from other entrepreneurs in temperament and style,
they frequently differ as to technology proposed. Zealots tend to
have a vision of the future and a sense of the technology that
will help solve problems. Their technologies tend to be radical
and large-scale and have broad impacts. They are impatient
and want quick results. The technologies they propose,
therefore, are preemptive in purpose.[32] They aim to shape the
future. They expect people in institutions to adjust to the
technology rather than vice-versa.

Because they are more sensitive to forces in their environment, the technology promoted by advocates is likely to be
incremental. In the long run, advocates might accomplish a
great deal in the way of change, but they would do so via
smaller steps. When the steps are small and less dramatic,
advocates are far more likely to achieve forward motion.
Zealous entrepreneurs, more often than not, try harder but
achieve less.

While these two styles represent abstractions from reality,
most entrepreneurs fall closer to one model than the other. In
our cases, the advocate entrepreneur is the dominant variety.
However, there are occasions when even advocates who
ordinarily are cautious in anticipating reactions will adopt a
zealot's stance. What makes entrepreneurs do what they do?

What are the stakes and motives of entrepreneurs?

Stakes come in many forms. The intensity of the stakes tends to determine whether the entrepreneur adopts a zealot or advocate style. The stakes can be economic (a builder promoting modular housing); electoral (an elected official using solid waste as a vehicle to gain reputation as an innovator and, thus, enhance his chances for retaining office); or organizational (administrative leaders using a new technology to expand their jurisdiction). The stakes can also be professional, relating to a sincere view based on professional understanding that a given innovation will improve services for a clientele. Thus, the particular innovative interest being pushed is a concrete manifestation of deeper values, and the entrepreneurial style is determined by a combination of the personality of the entrepreneur and the intensity with which a given innovation is identified with stakes such as the above. In both Syracuse and Rochester, the fate of certain innovations helped to determine the rise and fall of careers.

Bureaucratic entrepreneurs tend toward the advocacy style because they have general organizational interests to protect. To fight too hard for any one innovation may be harmful to the agency. This is especially true at the higher reaches of an organization. Lower down, an administrator can be a product champion, as was the computer specialist in the UFIRS case. When a particular innovation becomes the all consuming interest of an administrator, he identifies organizational stakes in survival, growth, and performance with a particular solution, and may actually hurt his organization if he fails. Alternatively, he may find that organizational interest requires his being expendable, as was the case with the school superintendent in the Syracuse Campus Plan and the head of the Rochester transportation authority in the Rochester dial-a-bus case.

Partisan or electoral interests can work against innovation as well as for it. In the Campus Plan case, the absence of entrepreneurship at the level of elected officials clearly contributed to its downfall. The scale of the technology was beyond the capacity of the organization. Politicians decided that this innovation was too divisive and sought to keep it off their decision agenda. In succeeding, they killed the plan and rendered the superintendent an expendable entrepreneur.

Nongovernmental entrepreneurs do not have bureaucratic or electoral stakes. Their interests tend to be economic, as in the housing cases. In the instance of the Syracuse modular housing businessman, these stakes went deeper. He truly believed that his technology was the best. He pushed until he ultimately failed when changes in the environment led to his going bankrupt.

As noted, adopters, implementers, and clients can serve as local entrepreneurs. Suppliers seek to be entrepreneurs behind the technology they wish to sell. Federal and state mission agencies may intervene in local processes, attempting to play an entrepreneurial role. However, our cases suggest that the optimal location for an entrepreneur is in local government. This does not obviate the utility of others playing entrepreneurial roles. It suggests that they are best seen as allies of an "inside" entrepreneur. Such an inside entrepreneur is in local government, understands the problem-solving perspective of the city, and can take a preferred innovation and translate it into terms that make it amenable to action: agenda setting, adoption, implementation, and incorporation. Our cases indicate that the entrepreneurs most able to fulfill this linkage function are top managers in line agencies. They appear to be in the most strategic position to play the entrepreneurial role under most conditions of local innovation. Ideally, they possess understanding of what is needed (performance gaps), what can be done (technology), and how to get decisions made in a local political environment.

Nonbureaucratic Entrepreneurship

Bureaucratic entrepreneurship is so dominant a theme in our cases that the exceptions deserve a special note. There were two cases where the entrepreneurs were legislators, one where the entrepreneur was the county executive, and two where entrepreneurship was shared between a private corporation and a state agency.

In the cable TV case, entrepreneurship centered in the city council. The absence of a bureaucratic entrepreneur in the early phases of the innovation process in this case is easily explained. There was no Syracuse agency set up to deliver a service called cable television. While cable TV was an incremental technology, objectively speaking, it was discontinuous in an organizational sense. Cable TV has been widely used in this country for years, but it did not reach Syracuse sooner because of the former FCC regulation excluding cable TV systems from the nation's 100 largest broadcast markets. The feasibility of the technology was never in question in the Syracuse case, and its complexity was no more a barrier to adoption than the complexity of a home television receiver was to diffusion of that technology. The key issue of the decision-making process was not the technology but whether the technology should be owned and operated by the city or by a profit-making or nonprofit private concern.

Certain legislators took the entrepreneurial initiative. They entered a governmental vacuum. There was no functional agency in existence. Their proposals led to the cable TV debate over whether a public agency should be created to serve as a user for the technology. When a technology is discontinuous, from the perspective of the local government (i.e., fully outside the existing tasks of the government), there is considerable leeway for action by others, including elected officials. Indeed, nothing may happen unless they act. It is noteworthy that, as the debate over cable TV intensified, bureaucracy appeared in an alliance role the legislative entrepreneurs reshaped the technology so as to make it useful to an existing line agency, the fire department.

In the Syracuse resource recovery case, the county executive, an elected official, attempted to take the lead within local government in moving this nonincremental innovation toward adoption. The explanation for this executive-centered, coalition-building process is more complicated than in the cable TV case. There was a Solid Waste Disposal Authority (SWDA) in existence. However, it lacked capacity to handle the technology at issue. This was another case of a technology that was discontinuous in terms of existing organizational structure. The feasibility of component technologies is generally established, and major manufacturers are involved in the resource recovery field. However, the performance of any plant of this size and scope is in many ways unique and dependent on local factors; therefore, its economic operation is somewhat uncertain. The technology is nonseparable and does not lend itself to trial implementation. Furthermore, it is a complex and esoteric piece of hardware. Like the shredder, it has a potentially broad impact on the local population, probably greater than that of the shredder because of its cost and highly visible site. Also its local environmental side effects are capable of generating strong interest and opposition on the part of a significant number of people.

Here was a $50 million effort of immense scale and technological complexity. The stakes of those who perceived themselves as being adversely affected by the siting of the facility were such as to make this a highly-politicized technology. This was a big technology and an important decision for the county, and the county executive felt that he had to take the lead on this particular innovation. An added element was the trouble that the existing organization was having with another recent adoption, the shredder, which was under attack on both technical and cost grounds. SWDA had all that it could handle in dealing with the shredder problem. If the county executive had not become the entrepreneur, resource recovery might not have been placed on the local decision-making agenda.

In the Monroe County resource recovery case, the entrepreneurial role was played by the county legislature's majority leader. The user agency was the Monroe County Public Works Department. Again, it appears that the technology was beyond the capacity of the organization. The public works department had but a limited role in solid waste management. The function of garbage pickup and disposal was largely an individual task of Rochester, suburban towns, and private firms.

In this case, the entrepreneur had to create a function for the county. This was essential because of the scale of the technology. The entrepreneur was aided in his efforts by his technical training and overlapping memberships. Not only was he an entrepreneur as a legislator, but he also had an entrepreneurial base in the Rochester Engineering Society

(RES), a citizens' interest group composed of members drawn from the Rochester technical community. RES was a strong proponent of the resource recovery plant.

The other exceptions to bureaucratic entrepreneurship lay in our housing cases. The function of housing is predominantly a private sector activity. However, a state agency, the Urban Development Corporation (UDC), united with private builders to promote innovations in these cases. UDC was created to help stimulate housing development in New York State. While UDC supplied funds and managerial talents, the proposals for most innovations came from the private sector. Thus, the explanation for this exception lies in the nature of this function as it operated in New York State.

To reiterate, the entrepreneur was not a line agency official in only a handful of cases. The county executive is an elected official, as are the legislative entrepreneurs. The scale of the technologies and their novelty, in terms of existing organization of urban functions, is almost certainly a critical variable. Discontinuous innovations are beyond the capacity of the relevant bureaucracy to assimilate in an incremental manner. Therefore, technology must result from entrepreneurship outside the line agency. Such entrepreneurship would appear to be the natural prerogative of the political leader. The other exceptions lie in a functional area where it is assumed, at least, that the private sector will innovate. Table 11 indicates who the entrepreneurs were in our various cases.

Bureaucratic Entrepreneurship

In the great majority of the cases in this study, an elected official did not seek to lead change. In fact, in some cases, such as Campus Plan, the mayor and legislators sought to avoid the issue. Politicians have little incentive to champion issues that involve taking risks that may cost them votes, and they rarely seek to lead where great effort will be required but few votes will be won. Many technological choices are of too low a visibility to interest politicians.

The Uniform Fire Incident Reporting System (UFIRS) is a good example of such a "nonpolitical" technological choice. It was an incremental innovation, and its impact was almost

Table 11

URBAN ENTREPRENEURS

Innovation	Syracuse	Rochester	Power Base
Campus Plan/ Project Unique	Superintendent of schools	Superintendent of schools	Administrative head of school district
Mini-pumper	Fire chief	Fire Chief	Head of fire department
Rapid Water	Fire chief		Head of fire department
OPTICOM	Fire chief		Head of fire department
UFIRS	Staff assistant to fire chief		Close relationship with head of fire department
Industrialized/ Modular Housing	Builder and UDC	Builder and UDC	In Syracuse, power base was UDC; builder had no real power base apart from UDC. In Rochester, main builder was technical advisor/consultant to UDC-GRI
SOVENT	UDC and local UDC manager		UDC (state organization with great powers and specific concern for housing innovation)
Team Policing	General Electric engineer, police chief, police captain	Director of Planning & Research (police captain who later became chief)	Police department planners supposed to come up with innovative solutions to crime problem. Had mandate for this from police chief.
School Resources and Information Program	Police chief		Head of police department
Solid Waste/ Shredders	Initially, Citizens Advisory Committee, especially staff director; then, Onondaga County Solid Waste Disposal Authority		Citizens Advisory Committee was composed of community leaders appointed by county executive. SWDA, an agency chartered by N.Y.S., was given authority for solid waste management in the county.

Table 11
(Continued)

Innovation	Syracuse	Rochester	Power Base
Resource Recovery	County executive; Carrier Corp.: Syracuse University. Mostly Carrier Corp. taking technical lead, with county executive political leader. Carrier was inside entrepreneur; county executive was outside salesman	County legislator who was majority leader of the Monroe County Legislature	Syracuse: Office of County Executive Rochester: the majority leader had party and legislative control. He also was a member of Rochester Engineering Society, the leading interest group pushing for the innovation.
Dial-a-bus	Executive director of authority	Executive director of authority	Administrative head of authority
Computerized Assessment	Private individual with skill in appraising real estate who later became town assessor		Expertise and fact that he represented a widely-shared interest
Cable Television	City legislator		Legislative constituency. Expertise of advisor/consultant John Fanetti

The bureaucratic entrepreneur was either the head of the organization or a subordinate supported by the head, with a power base dependent on position, constituency, and expertise. In most cases, entrepreneurship was bureaucracy-centered: fire, police, education, and transportation. The entrepreneur in solid waste/resource recovery was outside the user organization. This could relate to the discontinuity of the technology in Syracuse/Onondaga County. The issue on Cable TV was whether it should be a new public or private function. Housing had a business entrepreneur because it is a private function. However, UDC was influential in decision-making because, in addition to being banker, it had a high degree of public control over housing.

entirely within the Syracuse Fire Department. It was inexpensive, reversible without difficulty, not complex or esoteric, demonstrably feasible on the basis of implementation in other cities, and available from a willing supplier. It required only minor changes and fitted in well with the plans and activities of the fire department. In view of all this, it is not surprising that the department was able to make its decision internally, without involving political leaders or other external actors.

At the other end of the spectrum, some choices are highly visible and tend to be controversial and risky. In these instances, it is easier to leave the initiative with administrators who have greater expertise. The political leadership's attitude seems to be: let the agencies propose, and we will dispose. Unless the agencies take this entrepreneurial role, little seems to happen.

Why do agencies seek to adopt new technology? The answer would appear to lie in the interaction between the agency and its environment. That relationship, as seen by the entrepreneur, is more than the perception of a performance gap.[33] The important factors that motivate those who manage line agencies to seek change are: (1) who senses the performance gap, and (2) how forces in the environment of the agency influence the organization to act.

The environment of the local administrator is different from that of the elected leader. Elected leaders are responsive to constituents in the city or county who are voters. Agencies have constituencies at the local level, too, but they are also responsive to constituencies at the federal and state levels in their functional areas. Agency administrators may sense the same risks as do politicians, but they may be willing to take those risks because they have different incentives. Given the right circumstances, they will initiate a local government innovation process. For example, when a federal agency provided new funds for a demonstration project, as in the dial-a-bus cases, or when changes in the legal environment caused a productivity crunch, as in the fire cases, agency leaders took the lead. When they can, they will use their existing resources and authority. Where such resources and authority are insufficient, the best the entrepreneur can obtain is organizational commitment to get local government to adopt. In effect, the agency appeals to higher levels of the local system, as well as the state and federal governments. The entrepreneur thus succeeds in getting the innovation on the city's policy agenda. In this preadoption stage, however, there first must be a demand on the part of the subordinate unit, usually the agency.

The Syracuse mini-pumper illustrates how attributes of a technology can enhance organizational demand. Of the four firefighting innovations in Syracuse, the mini-pumper probably constituted the closest approximation to a nonincremental change. The standard pumper is a major piece of firefighting apparatus, and its use has been well established for years. The mini-pumper consists of a scaled-down version of the pumper. While the basic technology is not radically different from other pumpers, the manner in which the mini-pumper can be deployed represents a major departure from traditional modes of operation of fire departments in Syracuse, Rochester, and elsewhere.

The separable nature of the mini-pumper technology lent itself to trial implementation. In 1972, two prototypes were procured for testing at a cost of $22,000 each. Esotericism was not an issue since the innovation was largely designed in-house, using conventional components based on a truck used in rural areas for fighting brush fires. Because it originated in this manner and because the components were known and the prototypes were subjected to intensive testing, the mini-pumper, although not a previously proven innovation, quickly gained acceptance in the department. In effect, the organization helped to invent the mini-pumper and regarded it as its "baby." Cost and reversibility were somewhat intertwined in this case. Since the mini-pumper was a key element in a department-wide reorganization mandated by new state regulations, its implementation was part of the restructuring of the Syracuse Fire Department that, once completed, would be difficult and extremely costly to undo. On the other hand, the new state law that led to the reorganization of the department meant that return to the previous form of organization was not a viable option. Therefore, reversibility was probably not that important a concern to the decision makers. Cost of the mini-pumper, although far from negligible at $22,000 a unit, was assessed in the context of the overall departmental organization. The cost of the mini-pumper, as well as its associated labor costs, promised a considerable saving over the standard pumper that it partially replaced.

Initiating Innovation: Triggers in the Environment

What motivates some administrators to seek solutions to long-standing dilemmas, particularly solutions that involve technological innovations? One answer lies in the attitude of the administrator. Some are more willing to take risks than others. Some are more anxious to innovate than others. They see a performance gap and feel compelled to end it. Bureaucratic entrepreneurs with a zealous turn of mind will sometimes try to innovate irrespective of environmental conditions. Ordinarily, however, a positive attitude is not enough to initiate change. Even the best-intentioned administrators can be stymied by a system of constraints that is biased against innovation or by an organization that lacks the resources to innovate. Leaders can only act with dispatch and innovate under the right conditions. Under what conditions do administrators and their agencies initiate innovation?

In virtually every case in Syracuse and Rochester, an external stimulus, in the form of a threat or opportunity, was present. Sometimes strong, sometimes weak, this stimulus contributed to initiating serious problem solving by an organization together with advocacy by an entrepreneur. It was an action-forcing trigger. The nature of these stimuli is indicated in Table 12.

The fire cases reveal what might be considered the optimum external stimulus. New York State passed a law mandating a 40-hour work week for all firefighters. In Syracuse, the work week was 48 hours. The threat was direct: either services would have to be curtailed because of a shortage of manpower or new firefighters would have to be hired. Given the city's budgetary strictures, the cost of the latter would have been prohibitive, and curtailed services were politically unthinkable. The import and immediacy of the threat were such that there was no need nor time for a lengthy process of internal coalition building. There was consensus within the organization that a solution to this problem would have to be found by which service would be maintained. In Rochester, the fire department was already on a 42-hour work week. Therefore, the problem was less severe though still troublesome.

The external stimulus in Campus Plan was more vague. In

1965, as part of the Great Society program, Congress passed the Elementary and Secondary Education Act which provided considerable federal funding for local schools. Thus, there were incentives, or opportunities, at the local level to "think big" and act innovatively. At this time, the Syracuse City School District was faced with two problems: to replace deteriorated schools with new schools and to conform to the desegregation orders of the New York State Board of Regents. The opportunity to accomplish these objectives and, at the same time, improve education by way of innovation provided the stimulus for problem solving. This stimulus was vague, however, and triggered a disjointed local process of innovation.

As the Syracuse fire and education cases indicate, problems vary greatly in terms of their clarity and urgency. Of special importance is their salience for the agency and its top managers. Some problems are so big and involve so much change for the organization that no solution is possible without the interest of the top executive. Others are too small to excite the leader, but his agreement and support can be garnered by someone else in the organization who is interested in the problem. The management information problem was not at the pinnacle of the Syracuse fire chief's priorities, but it was important to a young staff assistant who got the chief's approval and moved ahead. In effect, it took a coalition of two, the specialist and the boss, within the fire department to initiate the process that led to the Uniform Fire Incident Reporting System.

Often a problem and an opportunity are perceived simultaneously. In the Rochester fire case, the stimulus was the city manager's request to the fire chief to increase productivity. The mini-pumper had been used in Syracuse for that purpose and presumably could help Rochester. However, since the severity of the threat in Rochester was not as great as it had been in Syracuse, the response was more modest.

Problems can be forced on an organization from outside, as in the previous examples, or they can be discovered as opportunities for creative innovation by someone inside the agency. In both Syracuse and Rochester, there were new people in charge of the police departments, men who had been placed there due to dissatisfaction with past management practices.

Table 12

EXTERNAL STIMULI IN THE SYRACUSE AND ROCHESTER CASES

Innovation	Syracuse	Rochester
Campus Plan/ Project Unique	Office of Education planning money and state directive regarding school integration. School building deterioration	Same as in Syracuse, except deterioration of school buildings was less of a problem
Mini-pumper	Change in state labor law	Change in state labor law and a general city fiscal crunch
Rapid Water	Change in state labor law	
OPTICOM	Change in state labor law	
UFIRS	Change in state labor law	
Industrialized/ Modular Housing	Active assistance from New York State Urban Development Corp.	Same as in Syracuse
SOVENT	Active assistance from New York State Urban Development Corp.	
Team Policing	Recommendations of a General Electric consultant and funds from Law Enforcement Assistance Administration	Rising crime rates
School Resource and Information Program	Serious disruption in schools	
Solid Waste Shredders	State environmental laws; grants from state and federal governments	
Resource Recovery	Interest of Carrier Corp.; availability of state funds; and state environmental laws	State environmental laws; state funds; interest of Rochester Engineering Society

Table 12
(Continued)

Innovation	Syracuse	Rochester
Dial-a-bus	Dept. of Health, Education, and Welfare and Dept. of Transportation funds; threat to survival of local mass transit	Dept. of Transportation funds; interest of MIT consultant
Computerized Assessment	State law; technical assistance funds; and local public protests about the fairness of existing assessment practices	
Cable Television	Change in federal and state regulations making it possible for Syracuse to adopt CATV	

They had mandates for change and were willing to take advantage of stimuli, whether internal or external to the department. The importance of the stimulus is to initiate a problem-solving process that provides an opening for the entrepreneur to get his ideas to the top of an organization's agenda. It helps to initiate action, but the action becomes innovation only when utilized by a local entrepreneur. It does not guarantee a decision to adopt. To be aware of problems and/or opportunities is one matter; taking action, especially innovative action, is another. Additional pressure from outside or persuasion by personnel from within the agency must be brought to bear to move from the initiation of a decision-making process to an actual decision to adopt.

Searching for Solutions

In rational models of organizational decision making, it is presumed that there will be a discrete search stage.[34] At this stage, problems would be carefully defined, and all options for solutions would be considered. Our study has indicated, however, that the rational model does not often work in practice. Organizations do not optimize; they adopt a solution that is satisfactory rather than one that is best because there is never enough time nor are there sufficient resources to find and evaluate that which is optimal.

Search processes vary in our cases from a snap judgment by the top executive to a long, drawn-out inquiry, as seen in Campus Plan, cable TV, and resource recovery. It is not at all clear that the amount of time it takes to decide on a solution has any relationship to a desire by proponents for an ideal result. It does appear, however, that the discussion is affected by characteristics of the innovation, particularly those that determine the amount of opposition that a proposal generates.

The most important factors in search procedures are who the searcher is and to whom he is listening. There is a thin line between organizational search and organizational planning. Organizations aware of problems are usually also aware of solutions. They usually have preferences, and often they have been talking for some time with particular providers of solutions such as manufacturers or consultants. All that is needed is the stimulus, or trigger, to facilitate action.

For example, the problem of fire trucks being slowed down by traffic lights was known long before the 1970s. The Syracuse Fire Department also knew about OPTICOM. OPTICOM is mainly a hardware system, and, while it is an innovation in Syracuse, it did not appear as a high-risk proposition. It represented an incremental change in fire department operations. It had been developed and was being marketed by a major industrial firm, and it had already been installed in a number of communities around the country. Syracuse officials were able to see the system in operation during a visit to St. Paul, Minnesota, and they were assured of its technical feasibility. The system was also a separable and reversible one. However, there was difficulty in moving toward a match between the problem and the solution. This was why the stimulus of the outside state law was so important.

Similarly, the problem of deteriorating schools was known to educational professionals in Syracuse. The educational park concept was regarded as a possible solution. Action was triggered by the prospect of outside money and state pressure on the local schools to do something about desegregation. In these cases, the real impact of the external force was to release pent-up energies within a local bureaucracy that had been waiting for a chance to move, to activate problem solving.

Who is searching along with the problem-solving bureaucracy becomes critical in determining possible options. Consider urban mass transit in Syracuse and Rochester. In both cases, the searching bureaucracy was a local transit authority. Who was searching with the organization? In Syracuse, it was the Metropolitan Commission on Aging (MCOA). In Rochester, it was the Massachusetts Institute of Technology and the Urban Mass Transportation Administration (UMTA). Consequently, Syracuse searched for a dial-a-bus that served a particular local constituency, the elderly and handicapped. Rochester officials, prompted by consultants and UMTA, sought a much more sophisticated dial-a-bus system that would serve as a national demonstration in demand-responsive mass transit and attract people from cars to buses. Thus, who searches at this early preadoption stage is all-important in determining what happens in later stages, because this is where the technology and problems are first "matched" and the design specified.[35]

Search loses its traditional meaning in many of our cases. What appears to be search is, in reality, rationalization and justification for decisions already implicitly made. In the case of school violence in Syracuse, there were two alternative solutions discussed by the school district and police department officials: installing electronic alarm systems or placing police in the schools. The hardware solution was not pushed. It might have been seriously considered had there been a manufacturer with a SCAN system in hand,[36] but no such manufacturer was present, and there was no inclination on anyone's part to wait for a rational search for alternatives to be conducted. The need was to act at once. The School Resources and Information Program offered a quick, relatively cheap, incremental solution to the problem. It was a managerial innovation with no hardware elements. Complexity was not an issue; nor was reversibility. The feasibility of the concept had only been proved on a limited basis prior to large-scale implementation in Syracuse, but the problem was viewed as being so critical that a system-wide trial was chosen rather than a limited trial. Initially, the concept was considered a temporary, stop-gap measure. However, a generally favorable public reaction and the discovery of long term intelligence functions of the program have led to its incorporation as a permanent aspect of the operations of the Syracuse Police Department and the city school system. The pattern, a temporary stop-gap measure and post hoc rationalization, was similar to that found in many of our cases.

It appears from our studies that administrative decision makers are constantly thinking about problems and possible solutions. There is plenty of talk, maybe even formal studies. (Studies of local solid waste problems and solutions in the two metropolitan areas go back decades.) Then, a stimulus appears on the scene, and the organization reacts by raising the priority of the problem and pressing for a solution. The solution or opportunity is thus shaped more by events, personalities, and who the administrator trusts than by any conscious search procedure. The Syracuse police chief listened to a local scientist from the General Electric Company who persuaded him that project management would be a good managerial technology for deploying police officers and for criminal investigation. His Rochester counterpart listened to an inside entrepreneur with a similar message. In Campus Plan, a school district planner's idea was embellished by input from numerous educational technology consultants often financed by federal money.

Is there an extensive search stage before a given solution is adopted? Or is a decision usually a hybrid of immediate search, previous planning, and public relations? More often than not, a quick search is made or a solution is taken off the shelf. Unless an administrator moves rapidly, he may miss an opportunity to solve a long-standing problem or implement a solution that he has wanted for years but could not previously hope to acquire. The search usually is of a kind that is incremental rather than synoptic, and one that has less to do with what is best (or even satisfactory) and more to do with how to take the innovation over the hurdles that lie between the emergence of idea and its ultimate incorporation.

Overcoming Opposition

Administrative entrepreneurs invariably face opposition. They are proposing change, and change usually causes trouble since it disrupts existing patterns of behavior. The more disruption, the greater the problems of effecting change. The entrepreneur must understand the characteristics of the technology, guage the nature of the opposition, consider the resources and strategies necessary to overcome the barriers that the opposition erects.

Opposition comes in two forms: passive and active. Passive opposition consists of rules, regulations, and other delay-producing factors in the social and legal system in which the innovating agency must operate. It also includes the existing weaknesses of the agency. The lack of money or personnel to formulate plans is a significant passive barrier to innovation. To separate passive from active barriers is often difficult. The active barriers are opponents working consciously to defeat the innovation. Frequently, they may attempt to make the passive barriers more difficult to overcome. Invariably, they seek to prevent the innovating agency from obtaining the necessary financial resources to adopt an innovation.

Active opponents can be found both inside and outside the agency. Among the internal opponents, none are more powerful than those in the management structure of the agency. If the leaders do not want an innovation, it will seldom be pushed forward. The Crime Control Team idea went nowhere in Syracuse until a new police chief took command. The team-policing concept would have had little chance in Rochester had it not had the strong backing of the police chief. Here was an innovation that reduced the status and functions of the detectives, a powerful element in the departments. In another example, a modular housing proposal seemed to be finding its way toward adoption by the Syracuse Housing Authority. Then, a change in political administration altered the leadership of that agency, and the new leadership opposed the proposed innovation.

Campus Plan attempted to bring about radical change in education on a system-wide basis. The concept was costly, and its feasibility had not been demonstrated. There was no relevant experience from other settings that could serve as convincing evidence of the plan's viability. It was separable, but not in a way that lent itself to low-risk trial adoption. One campus could be built to accommodate pupils from one section of the city. The campus that was proposed for initial implementation was estimated to cost $19.7 million for the capital cost only, and its construction would have inevitably led to abandonment of the existing neighborhood schools. While this campus could serve as a testing ground for the campuses planned for other sections of the city, it would constitute an essentially irreversible change for one part of the city.

Campus Plan was not initially complex or particularly esoteric, but it became more complex and difficult to understand as it developed. A number of hardware innovations, particularly computer-assisted instruction, were incorporated into the proposal without much consideration being given to their acceptability. A more politically volatile urban innovation is hard to imagine. Opposition was strong and active. The superintendent of schools faced an outside opponent who became an inside opponent when he was elected to the Board of Education. Privy to the plans of the educational bureaucrats, he was capable of quickly producing counter-strategies to the pro-innovation strategies they devised. A multiheaded organization is particularly prone to access by groups opposing innovation. Given a multitude of passive yet powerful barriers, a little active opposition can nip an innovation in the bud or so warp the planning effort as to make what is finally adopted hardly innovative.

A critical error of the Campus Plan entrepreneur was to concentrate innovations in ways that were nonseparable. When the facility innovation was defeated, the programmatic changes went down with it. In Rochester, the facility was treated as one of a number of innovations. Opponents could focus on one or two parts of Project Unique, but they also found other parts they liked. The separability dimension of the innovation permitted the entrepreneur to concentrate on the areas in which he had support, sacrificing those parts of the package that lacked support or had strong opposition. In effect, he diffused his opposition by the way he presented Project Unique.

Depending upon the degree and influence of opposition, considerable resources may have to be mobilized by entrepreneurs. The stronger the opposition, the more strength the proponents must have. This is especially true in getting the necessary financial resources to procure a particular innovation. For example, in the adoption of UFIRS, which cost $2500, the Syracuse Fire Department could go from planning to the adoption decision on its own. With OPTICOM, which cost over $600,000, the department had to go to the political levels for the adoption decision. Thus, UFIRS could be decided largely in an intraorganizational framework, whereas OPTI-COM represented more of an interorganizational process. One is agency decision making; the other is local government decision making.

Financial resources are necessary to adopt many innovations, and political resources are required to obtain financing. Thus, an entrepreneur who succeeds in getting agency commitment to a small-scale innovation in the preadoption phase may well succeed in getting adoption. The decision-making process on adoption stops there. Organizational commitment and adoption are synonymous in cases such as Rapid Water and UFIRS in Syracuse and the mini-pumper in Rochester. For larger-scale technology, however, organizational commitment simply ends a preadoption phase and ushers in a separate stage of decision making involving elected officials. Organizational commitment is not enough under such circumstances. Bureaucratic entrepreneurship perforce requires advocacy within the local community.

6
Obtaining Adoption

If the costs of innovation are minimal, the decision-making cycle can be relatively short and closed. Once a chief executive approves an innovation, placing it on the agency's agenda, adoption has occurred. The bureaucracy has the necessary resources and adopts on its own. For innovations of great cost or high visibility, however, the decision process will generally involve a larger set of interests, even to the point where top elected leadership preempts agency activity. Such cases may well require community-wide decision making in which agencies seek public support for adoption. Legitimacy may be at issue even when costs are not. The fact that a technology is new often requires affirmative decisions by those with electoral-based authority. Thus, this chapter deals primarily with adoptions at a level beyond the agency. In these instances, bureaucracy cannot adopt officially unless others permit it to do so.

With few exceptions, most of the innovations that we studied cost more than could be absorbed within the existing budgets of the agencies. Consequently, while the agency was in the entrepreneurial lead, it had to seek adoption in a relatively open system. It had to go through a local political process to obtain the necessary money and legal authority to adopt. Thus, the agency becomes involved in coalition building. These are bureaucracy-centered coalitions. The size of the coalitions, the strategies utilized to form and maintain them, and the importance of federal and state activities vary among the functional areas studied. How well an agency succeeds in acquiring financial resources for an innovation depends on what might be called its entrepreneurial resources and how it utilizes them.

Resources

Entrepreneurial resources are related to an agency's overall capacities and power base. It is clear that some agencies start from a stronger advocacy position than others, regardless of what they seek to acquire. There are many resources that make up such a power base.[37] An organization that may be weak in one respect can be strong in another and thus compensate. However, an agency in most resource categories is probably doomed to frustration or, at least, to thinking small and in conventional and incremental terms.

Legislative Mandates

Some agencies have legislative mandates that give them room to maneuver, while others are extremely constrained. Consider two organizations in Syracuse that appear to be similar types of governmental bodies. They are both authorities: Central New York Regional Transportation Authority (RTA) and Onondaga County Solid Waste Disposal Authority (SWDA). On the surface, these two authorities might seem alike. In reality, they operate from very different power bases. Both have state enabling acts, but there the similarity ends and differences appear. SWDA has no tax support; RTA does. SWDA serves one county; RTA serves a multicounty region. The enabling legislation of SWDA allows other entities to provide similar services in its jurisdiction; RTA exercises virtually a monopolistic control of public transportation services in its region. The county executive appoints the head of SWDA; the director of RTA is appointed by the governor. This comparison indicates the greater leverage of RTA.

The New York State Urban Development Corporation (UDC) probably represents the ultimate example of a legislative mandate working on behalf of urban innovation. The legislation creating UDC in 1968 not only specifically endorsed technological innovaton in housing construction, but it also authorized UDC to circumvent normal housing development procedures to move with unusual speed. In addition, in its early years, UDC had almost limitless funding. Considering the scope of the housing cases in Syracuse and Rochester, the innovations were adopted with few hitches.

Constituencies

What is true of authorities is equally true of line agencies. The differences are considerable, and they matter when it comes to innovation. Agencies start with different mandates, and they work in vastly different constituency environments. The constituencies of some agencies stretch no further than the city environs, while other local agencies have "friends" in Albany and Washington. Constituencies vary in size, in the intensity of their interest in a local agency, and in their attitude toward the agency. If the agency has a constituency that wants the agency to expand its services (e.g., the elderly and the handicapped wanted a more extensive dial-a-bus operation in Syracuse), it has a fairly good environment in which to think big and innovatively as long as it adheres to the constituency's interests. If the constituency includes opponents or functional rivals, the agency will avoid innovations that may bring it into conflict with the opposing forces in its environment.

Perhaps the worst situation was exemplified by the Onondaga County SWDA. This organization was formed by the state at the request of the county to provide needed regionalization of waste disposal. Because local politicians anticipated that many actions of the authority would be unpopular, especially locating landfill sites, SWDA was purposely isolated from local popular control. It was answerable only to the county executive who appointed its board members and chairman. This arrangement proved satisfactory as long as the county executive, a Republican, was allied to the elected officials of the city and the members of the county legislature. However, the city's leadership changed, and the new Democratic administration was suspicious of SWDA, which it saw as a Republican pawn. In addition, SWDA alienated a number of members of the county legislature whose districts were considered for landfill sites. Thus, SWDA, with a necessary but unpopular mission, found itself with an unfriendly and sometimes hostile constituency. Since it did not have the power to levy taxes, it required subsidies from the county legislature in addition to user fees in order to cover expenses. Hence, the lack of friends and existence of enemies has led to a very real possibility that SWDA will be terminated and another agency, one with a more powerful base, will replace it. The lesson to be learned here is that having authority on paper does not necessarily mean that an agency is powerful.

The absence of a supportive constituency for urban mass transit in Rochester prompted an official of the mass transit agency in that city to complain, "We are an authority without any authority." It is noteworthy that its sister agency in Syracuse consciously used dial-a-bus to build its local constituency, whereas Rochester did not.

With mixed results, UDC tried to build constituencies by making established local housing interests UDC subsidiaries. The Metropolitan Development Association in Syracuse and UDC-Greater Rochester, Inc., were involved by UDC in such functions as site selection and design. This state-local alliance helped to promote relatively swift adoption of UDC's housing projects in the two cities. Thus, in its way, UDC had to engage in a local decision-making process to legitimize its techno-logical choices. It did not have to go through a local legislature for funding, but it had to assure local housing interests that the state was being responsive to (and responsible for) local needs.

Professional Expertise

Agencies also differ in their expertise. More precisely, they differ in terms of how others perceive their expertise. If elected officials and the public believe that the agency management knows something that they do not know, they will "leave it to the experts." Fire and police chiefs are given a deference that the school superintendent is not. The body of knowledge underlying police and fire services may be no more certain than that behind education, but there is a tendency to go along with police and fire officials, whereas educational authorities are questioned closely. This may be because fire and police represent a personal security dimension of urban life. They also have more glamour than other urban agencies. The television networks have numerous programs that chronicle the exploits of police in solving crimes. There is "Emergency," a program that displays the heroics of firefighters. Even locally, the police and firefighters receive a great deal of media coverage by virtue of what they do. This news coverage, which is usually favorable, keeps these functions before the public eye. However, while public visibility is important, public understanding is equally important. We may not know how best to educate our child, but we believe we know what kind of a job the schools are doing. If Johnny cannot read, it must be the fault of the professional educators.

Morale and Cohesion

Related to expertise is the general morale, or cohesion, of an agency. If there is high esprit de corps and everyone is working in harmony toward common objectives, the agency will be in a good position to enter any contest for innovation. Its position will be weakened, however, if it is torn by union dissension, petty rivalries, and the special interests of autonomous subordinate units.

Match between Agency and External Stimulus

Legislative mandates, constituency environments, expertise, and morale are mainstays of an agency's advocacy resources. Such resources constitute a baseline, a starting point. They affect the ability of an agency to deal with the external threat or opportunity.

In eight of the cases studied, the fire and police departments were the involved agencies, and they had missions and capabilities that closely matched the demands of the external stimulus. In the dial-a-bus cases, new agencies came into existence. These agencies had missions and capabilities sufficient to allow them to pursue the external opportunity (grants from local and federal sources) and to deal with deteriorating local mass transportation. In the computerized assessment case, the Manlius assessor had to be replaced to make room for a person who could deal with such external factors as a new state law and state technical assistance, developing these into an innovation. In the SOVENT plumbing case, there was jurisdictional rivalry. There was no agency that could claim and enforce clear responsibility. While this was a matter of housing, and thus fell under UDC jurisdiction, it was also a problem for some local agencies. In this instance, the others chose to contend. SWDA is proving incapable of meeting the problems and opportunities in its environment. It remains to be seen whether the similar agency in Rochester will do any better. It is a newly-established bureau of the Monroe County Department of Public Works and is directly responsible to the county legislature.

It is clear that some agencies *begin* with a base of political legitimacy and support while others have to *obtain* support. Any agency can *lose* support by the decisions it makes. The resources mentioned—legislative mandates, constituency, expertise, morale—do not, by themselves, guarantee a congruence between the external stimulus and the organizational response, much less a response that converts the problem/opportunity into an innovation. The most critical resource buttressing and directing all the rest is administrative leadership. The kind of leadership that must be demonstrated is not strictly managerial. It requires entrepreneurship in the political environment of the contemporary city.

Strategies

What strategies[38] does the bureaucratic entrepreneur use to get an innovation adopted? There are several. He markets the innovation. He uses outside funding. He demonstrates the innovation to the right people at the right time. He rallies community interest groups to his side and persuades the communication media to work with him rather than against him. In effect, he builds a coalition of support around the innovation in the hope that enough momentum can be gathered through mini-decisions to push through the big decision of governmental adoption.

Marketing

It takes one kind of talent to manage and another to market.

The bureaucratic entrepreneur who wants to adopt an innovation of significant scale is going to have to market his ideas. This is certainly the case with costly hardware innovations.

For example, adoption of the techniques that helped modernize the Syracuse Fire Department was largely attributable to the fire chief's marketing talent. He turned the threat represented by a new state law into an opportunity. He promoted the mini-pumper and other equipment innovations in productivity terms that the mayor and common council understood. He argued that spending money for new technology was a good alternative to greater, long-term manpower expenses. He even marketed the mini-pumper to his fellow professional, the Rochester fire chief.

Moderation

Moderation is difficult for bureaucratic entrepreneurs with a streak of zealotry. It was difficult for the Syracuse school superintendent who sought radical change. The Rochester superintendent accomplished more, incrementally, with moderation.

Moderation is a strategy that is especially important for bureaucratic entrepreneurs who approach local officials from a somewhat elevated position. For example, the head of the Syracuse transit authority legally did not have to go through the Syracuse political process to achieve the adoption of dial-a-bus since he already had a broad, state-backed mandate. However, he felt it wise to have local political support if his agency was ultimately to succeed. He needed the informal, if not official, backing of political leaders. To gain it, he linked dial-a-bus with their interests. Given the increasing proportion of elderly people in the city, the elected officials in Syracuse were happy to show their concern for these voters. Dial-a-bus was an ideal technology from this point of view.

The Syracuse application, in addition, was incremental rather than radical in its impact on the transportation field. To avoid technological complexity, dial-a-bus used rather conventional hardware, although, for a variety of reasons, a supplier was not immediately available. Similar systems had been employed in other communities throughout the United

States. Since a limited trial adoption was a logical and easy first step by virtue of the separability of the technology, the feasibility of dial-a-bus in the Syracuse environment was quickly established. Although dial-a-bus provides an important service and is visible to the general public, its impact on most people outside its immediate constituency and its association with deeply held public values is slight.

Although costs were relatively high for the type of service that the innovation offered, the availability of federal funds and the existence of a clear-cut client group helped to counteract this problem. Reversibility was also a simple matter with dial-a-bus. Implementing the system did not foreclose any significant options. The head of the Syracuse authority was conscious of his need to cultivate political support, and he made certain that local elected officials shared the publicity spotlight when dial-a-bus was introduced, even though he did not have to do so.

In contrast, Rochester transit officials did not exercise moderation in their selection of a much more sophisticated and complex dial-a-bus system. To achieve adoption, this system needed a critical linkage with county legislators who would help fund its operating costs. They saw little in dial-a-bus that justified their votes. They regarded it more as an instrument of outside desires (i.e., the technocratic interests of MIT and the national demonstration concerns of UMTA) than as a service to their constituency, most of whom preferred and used cars rather than the dial-a-bus service.

UDC did not exercise moderation in the SOVENT case, at least in the opinion of the Onondaga County Health Department. Viewed from the perspective of these local officials, UDC was overbearing. UDC's efforts to override local wishes in this case has left a legacy of mistrust, and Onondaga County officials are not unhappy that UDC has had to withdraw from some of its local projects.

The superintendent of schools in Syracuse was hardly overbearing, but he appeared insensitive to local political leaders. He regarded education as above politics. His lack of enthusiasm in dealing with elected officials stood in sharp contrast to his zeal in embracing educational consultants in developing the plan.

Moderation in the case of the Rochester Fire Department's adoption of only one mini-pumper was a strategy of a different kind. The firefighters' union, fearing that more mini-pumpers meant fewer firefighters, was delighted to impress the departmental entrepreneur with the virtues of moderation in this case.

Minimizing Local Costs

Local costs can be minimized in two ways: in real dollar terms or in appearance only. That is, the entrepreneur can bring local costs down by shifting some of the costs to outsiders such as the federal or state governments, or he can make these costs seem lower than they actually are by the way he presents them. While the fire cases suggest that a strong local coalition without outside resources may be sufficient to gain adoption in certain instances of extreme environmental threat, many of the other cases forcefully argue the need for an outside funding opportunity as a catalyst. An intergovernmental coalition built along functional lines can help to generate a local coalition by transferring front-end costs to higher levels of government.

Intergovernmental aid. Outside funding for planning kept Campus Plan on the city's adoption agenda for over three years in the late 1960s. One planning grant led to another, adding up to $360,000, a fact which suggests that the skill of the superintendent of schools was greater in building an intergovernmental coalition than one on the home front. Underlining this observation was the fact that the superintendent had more outside money than he could effectively spend. The money did keep the project alive, but only in the planning phase. When federal funds were curtailed, Campus Plan had to be shelved.

The large capital expenditures in the Syracuse dial-a-bus, the proposed steam station, and shredder cases would not have been possible without grants by the state and federal governments. In computerized assessment, state funding gave the town board the incentive to seriously consider adopting this innovation.

It is noteworthy that the city of Syracuse has established an office under the mayor specifically charged with helping agencies to obtain grants from Albany and Washington. In this sense, the mayor acts as a broker in the coalition process. He may play a more strategic role in an intergovernmental than a local coalition.

The Rochester situation is similar with respect to the importance of outside money. Intergovernmental aid forced adopters to think seriously about an innovation. Project Unique had money from the U.S. Office of Education; dial-a-bus had money from the Department of Transportation; and team policing had funds from the Police Foundation and the Law Enforcement Assistance Administration.

Transferring costs forward. Another way of minimizing immediate local costs is to transfer them forward through bonding. In this way, the problem of local payment for an item is postponed. This suggests the related tactic of obscuring costs. Bonding obscures costs, not only by transferring payment to a later time but also by making it easy to ignore the costs. The tactic of obfuscation can be seen in the way would-be entrepreneurs present costs to decision makers. They present operating costs in terms of annual expenses rather than the total cost of operating the innovation over its lifetime. This tactic also evades dealing with the impact of inflation.

The cases show how costs can be made to appear to be savings. In advocating mini-pumpers and other fire innovations, the Syracuse bureaucratic entrepreneur advanced them as money-saving devices. Campus Plan's total costs were also kept out of sight as much as possible. School district planners rarely mentioned that one effect of adoption would be a 40 percent increase in the district's operating budget.

The lesson is clear from the cases: innovation usually costs money. In the long run, it may save money or produce user benefits worth the added operating costs. However, since local politicians react primarily to immediate pressures, administrative entrepreneurs are advised to find ways to shift costs upward, forward—or "under the rug."

Demonstrations

It has often been noted that successful large-scale public demonstrations of new technologies are important in gaining support of elected officials and clients.[39] This was true in our studies, although we found that not all innovations are amenable to demonstration. In the computerized assessment case, a skeptical town board was not convinced of the merits of the innovation until it assembled in Albany and was shown printouts of the assessment model. Only after the members were convinced of the equity of the model, in terms of the impacts of reassessment on them as well as on powerful constituents, did they decide to adopt the innovation. Dial-a-bus was expanded in Syracuse after a pilot project revealed considerable demand for the service. The Syracuse Fire Department sought to use a two-year demonstration of OPTICOM on a busy street in Syracuse as a basis for expanding the system city-wide. A trial implementation established the feasibility and acceptance of team policing in both Rochester and Syracuse. Demonstrations are usually regarded as mechanisms for gaining constituencies for those technologies. This proved to be the case for Project Unique in Rochester, but not for the Rochester dial-a-bus. In Rochester, the dial-a-bus demonstration showed that there was an insufficient local demand for the sophisticated program and also revealed serious technical problems in the system.

A federally-funded demonstration in Madison, Wisconsin, influenced the decision of SWDA to adopt solid waste shredders in Onondaga County. A citizens' advisory group on solid waste visited Madison and was so impressed with the shredder technology that it helped persuade the county executive that this was a solution to favor. Although the technology did not lend itself to a small-scale local demonstration, the Madison shredder served the same purpose.

While the shredder was not necessarily a revolutionary or radical innovation in solid waste management, it certainly represented more than an incremental change for the manner in which Onondaga County handled its solid waste. When the idea first arose in the Syracuse context, only a handful of manufacturers were involved in the business, and shredders hardly could have been regarded as a proven technology. The characteristics of the technology that contributed to the lengthy disputes surrounding its implementation were its cost, the difficulty of establishing its feasibility (particularly its cost-effectiveness compared to alternative technologies), and its lack of susceptibility to trial implementation. Due to the large capital outlays required, commitment to shredder technology seems to have been viewed as essentially irreversible by most of those involved in the decision-making process at the time.

Two compensations for these factors helped to make adoption and implementation of the shredder possible: some solution to the pressing problem of solid waste disposal appeared necessary to most adopters; and the primary alternative technology of incineration suffered from many of the same handicaps (high cost, irreversibility, nonseparability) as did the shredder. The Wisconsin demonstration helped to sell the idea to the county executive and SWDA, but a local demonstration would have been useful in allowing them to sell the idea to the city which bitterly fought adoption of the shredders.

Some technologies such as resource recovery are not demonstrable beforehand, at least at the local site. Thus, an entire range of problems, from technical to political, has to be anticipated, and objections to adoption overcome. In Syracuse, the entrepreneur, with the help of Carrier Corporation, could not do this. In Rochester, with the help of a local professional engineering society, the entrepreneur could.

Using the Mass Media

Editorial support and favorable news coverage from the mass media can help an entrepreneur to achieve the necessary coalition of official adopters. Bureaucratic leaders with a keen sense of their marketing roles are generally aware of the need to build good will with the local press and radio and television stations. Mass media can be used to advantage in specific cases where there is a need to reach political leadership through the public. For example, from the time he took office, the head of the Syracuse transit authority went out of his way to be responsive to the need of the local press for information. He became accustomed to providing news to a local newspaper reporter who called him each morning. Such actions build close relationships that can result in favorable press when an administrator needs it to persuade reluctant politicians. In contrast, the Rochester transportation authority head did not choose to allocate his time to building good press relations.

The chief of the Syracuse Fire Department is especially adept at using the press to forge a winning coalition among political adopters. He regularly holds press conferences and makes appearances in the newspaper offices. He has little trouble gaining access to the press or local television to reach the public with a given message. He made excellent use of the press to get an adoption decision in the mini-pumper case. The funding proposal was before the common council and was in trouble, having been tabled. Shortly after this development, a fire in Syracuse did extensive damage to a large apartment complex. At the scene of the fire, the chief attacked the common council before reporters and television cameras, declaring that if the fire department had had the equipment that it was requesting the fire could have been contained. He further implied that common council inaction was jeopardizing the lives of his men and the citizens of Syracuse. At the next meeting of the common council, the bonding resolution for mini-pumpers and other equipment was unanimously passed, and several councilors attributed their change of heart to the media accounts of the chief's complaint.

If the media can help, it can also hurt. Campus Plan was a complex package of proposals. The newspapers chose to highlight the ones that were most politically volatile such as the impact on neighborhood schools, busing, and the technological approach to teaching involving individually programmed instruction. Editorials unfavorable to the plan appeared at critical points during the course of the debate. While the media cannot be blamed for the defeat of Campus Plan, the newspapers undoubtedly added to a tide of public opposition to the proposal. The metropolitan media have the capacity to broaden the constituency and sway opinion on an issue. It is no wonder that bureaucratic entrepreneurs seek to make the media allies in their coalition-building efforts.

Using Community Groups

As entrepreneurs seek to use the press, so they attempt to

array citizens' groups behind their adoption proposals. Sometimes they succeed (e.g., Project Unique in Rochester); sometimes they fail (e.g., Campus Plan in Syracuse).

While most entrepreneurs speak the rhetoric of citizen participation, they actually are often ambivalent about community groups.[40] This is especially the case when they have strong professional identification. As government officials and professionals, they have the position and training that suggests to them that they know best what clients need. Their technical leanings thus are often at odds with the necessities of political entrepreneurship, and attempts at participation often become somewhat suspect, appearing to be an effort in cooptation rather than a genuine sharing of decision-making power. They wish to develop their plans first and then enlist the support of groups if and when they are needed.

Such a strategy may work in certain functions where clients are widely diffused and seldom cohesive, as in police and fire services. In those functions, it indeed may be difficult to stimulate clientele support, even if such support is desired. The Rochester firefighters' union tried and failed to stimulate community action against adoption of the mini-pumper. For functions that are presumably geared to specific groups, however, more than token involvement is essential in building an adoption coalition. In the Syracuse dial-a-bus case, there was genuine involvement of clientele groups representing the elderly and handicapped in the processes of agenda-setting and matching that preceded adoption. This was not true in the Rochester dial-a-bus case; consequently, adoption there is on the brink of failure. It is noteworthy that the clientele group in the Syracuse case had genuine power to assert its claims on the authority. It literally bought into the local decision-making process in urban mass transit with an independent source of funds, an HEW grant. In considering these community linkages, one important variable is the exchange between client and entrepreneur. What price does the local entrepreneur have to pay for clientele support of what he wants in adoption? Is he willing to pay the price? The Syracuse entrepreneur apparently was; the Rochester entrepreneur was not. To their detriment, bureaucratic entrepreneurs who hold strong views are likely to attempt preemptive participation.

The danger with cooptation strategies is that enlarging the coalition too much, too soon, may let in a force bent on destroying an adoption process or drastically changing the type of innovation that the entrepreneur wants. The Syracuse educational entrepreneur made this mistake with one champion of neighborhood schools. After placing him on an advisory committee, the entrepreneur found him using inside information to enlarge an anti–Campus Plan coalition. In Rochester, the educational entrepreneur took the risks of broad participation, but he did so in two steps. First he enlisted the help of elite community groups rather than actual clients. He entered into planning with Eastman Kodak, the University of Rochester, and the Industrial Management Council. Then, after the core group had decided what it wanted, he broadened the coalition to include clients (e.g., parents). The lesson to be learned is that an entrepreneur does not build a coalition randomly, but does so sequentially, starting with those whose influence is greatest. Winning these elite groups provides a core of support that makes it possible to move to the next steps, clientele and general community support. The Syracuse entrepreneur did not do this.

The same strategy was used in the Rochester resource recovery case. The Rochester Engineering Society was an elite, profession-based citizens' group. It served as a catalyst and intermediary, helping the legislative entrepreneur win broader support from the community for adoption of the innovation. Carrier Corporation is also an elite institution, but it did not have the credibility with the public that the Rochester Engineering Society had. After all, Carrier wanted to build the resource recovery unit because it had an obvious vested interest. Hence, entrepreneurs working with elite interest groups must give attention to the credibility that such intermediaries have with the public they are trying to influence.

Conclusion

In conclusion, it can be stated that adoption is coalition building by another name. For small technologies within the existing authority and resources of agencies, adoption is possible by organizations alone. But most significant innovations do not fit such conditions. They must be honed down to scale or else passed by as being beyond the capacities of the local buyer. Alternatively, as we have discussed in this chapter, the organization may alter its boundaries to enable it to adopt a technology it wants. In the extreme case (cable TV), where no organization exists, a new receptacle is created by the political levels to make adoption possible. Ordinarily, the organization seeks to expand its authority and financial resources to enable it to acquire the innovation. This necessitates positive action by those entities which can provide such items to the local organization. Such resource providers are at the local level as well as the national and state levels. The agency leaders become entrepreneurs. They build a coalition that is horizontal (local) and vertical (intergovernmental) which permits them to expand to match the innovation desired. Where they succeed, adoption by the city allows them to go forward, and they can legitimately begin the next phase of urban innovation, that of implementation.

7
Implementation:
Completing the Coalition

As adoption of a new technology requires coalition building, so does implementation. However, the emphasis of the coalition building changes. Elected officials become less an object of bureaucratic attention and strategy. In their place, new focal points emerge: suppliers, clients, and employees. While bureaucracy seeks to hold the allegiance of politicians, it also attempts to build a distinct coalition that is geared to implementation. At the adoption stage, entrepreneurship falls to the leader of the organization who must establish linkages with elected officials and other resource providers. During implementation, entrepreneurship is often delegated to an official below top management. The task of the implementing entrepreneur is to guide the innovation into an operating reality while the top people move on to the next crisis. The line between adoption and implementation is extremely blurred in some of our cases. This is because federal demonstrations become implementation processes, in effect. Some local money may be involved. Hence, there is a form of adoption, but federal officials share the risk. In doing so they may make implementation more difficult, as the local implementing entrepreneur is more concerned about keeping Washington happy than mending urban fences.

Target Groups

What are some problems in building an implementing coalition? What strategies have bureaucratic entrepreneurs used to overcome them?

Employees

The people who actually build new technologies or put them into use are employees at the lower echelons of bureaucracies, yet they have the power to delay and sometimes defeat an adoption decision reached by top management and/or the city's political leadership. For the most part, such employee resistance is born of a fear of learning new routines, losing status, or even being put out of work. Often the fear is well founded.

In the Syracuse fire cases, several older firefighters saw the new equipment as mildly threatening. They certainly saw it as causing them problems. They liked the old ways and regarded retraining as a chore. Resistance to the mini-pumper reached the point of being a union issue in Rochester largely because of fears of job losses. In the Syracuse and Rochester team policing cases, many police officers deeply resented what they perceived as the creation of an elite corps within the department; and those most threatened, the detectives, strongly opposed it. In the Syracuse housing cases, unionized plumbers opposed the introduction of new building techniques that undercut their prerogatives.

The older firefighters in Syracuse grumbled and suffered some morale problems, but there is no evidence of outright resistance, in large part because of the strategies of the fire chief. In Rochester, the fire chief did run into heated union opposition, and this probably was a factor in halting the acquisition of more mini-pumpers.

There was also resistance in the police cases. In Syracuse, the police officers who first joined crime control teams found themselves ostracized by former colleagues who had not been chosen. Dispatchers at times failed to understand and sometimes ignored special instructions from the chief of police that the crime control team should not be sent on certain types of noncriminal calls. In Rochester, there were similar instances of noncooperation on the part of those who felt threatened by the change. Attempts by middle managers to hinder the operation of the Coordinated Team Patrols, such as assigning the most dilapidated patrol cars to CTP units, were common.

In the Syracuse housing cases, efforts to innovate were met with resentment by workers. When unionized plumbers learned that industrialized techniques had produced a factory-built plumbing system, they forced UDC to have this system disassembled when it arrived on the site and reassembled by them. In the SOVENT case, a two-by-four was discovered inserted into a four-inch sewer pipe at a critical turn in the system. Did the opposition to SOVENT (the plumbers) seek to sabotage the innovation? There was no proof, but plenty of suspicion.

To most users of plumbing systems (i.e., residents of the buildings in which they are installed) SOVENT would not seem like a very radical innovation. Few residents would be aware of its existence unless they were specifically informed about it. To plumbers who install it, contractors who pay for it, and regulatory agencies that must certify its use in construction, however, it represents a sufficiently large departure from a conventional plumbing system to qualify as a nonincremental change. From the perspective of the professional arena in which construction decisions are made, SOVENT is a significant departure from the norm.

In general, SOVENT does not seem particularly costly, complex, or esoteric. Given the conservative nature of the construction industry, however, it might have been perceived as esoteric by some. The system in Syracuse was considered by UDC to be separable and reversible, with the case at issue a trial implementation. If the Syracuse installation succeeded, UDC may have used SOVENT in other parts of the state. However, large-scale construction projects are rarely seen as trials. At the local level, the character of decision making was strongly influenced by the fact that, even if the installation was regarded by some as a trial implementation, it represented a substantial investment in itself. At the Syracuse trial site, it was not easily reversible, and future residents were going to have to live with it. Thus, proof of technical feasibility is a more sensitive issue in construction than in other types of trial implementation, and the apparent lack of such proof, despite the claims of manufacturers, was a key problem in the SOVENT case. The construction industry poses some special barrier to technologies whose characteristics would otherwise make them relatively easy to introduce.

To reiterate, the support of employees, whether they are direct staff of the agency or indirect contractual employees, is essential in the implementation of new technology. If such support is not present at the time of adoption, it must be obtained during the implementation phase. Moreover, such support must be more than a spirit of cooperation. It has to have a technical base. The enthusiastic support of employees or contractors who are ill-equipped to perform a given task may not be helpful during implementation. In the Rochester dial-a-bus case, for example, the technical capacity to manage this sophisticated project apparently was not to be found in the authority. The implementers in charge were a group of MIT specialists in demand-responsive systems. While their technical competence was undeniable, their sensitivity to the local political scene was wanting. Implementing a local transit project in Rochester from Cambridge, Massachusetts, was hardly desirable. This contributed to problems in acquiring the essential local coalition around dial-a-bus.

Suppliers

The key role of suppliers as coalition members is obvious. If the suppliers are manufacturers of hardware and are not present at adoption, they must be recruited afterward. Enlisting them is not always easy. Many companies are not attracted to what they perceive as the nonmarket of urban America.

The Syracuse transit agency promoting dial-a-bus found that the company it had expected to supply the specially equipped minibuses had opted out of the dial-a-bus business. Months passed before a replacement could be found and approved. Even then, the chosen firm could not deliver the specified equipment within the resources originally allocated. To keep within the budget, the specifications were revised, and one of the more innovative features, the teleprinters used for dispatching, was dropped.

A similar problem occurred in the modular and industrialized housing cases. In both Syracuse and Rochester, the demand for housing created by the abundance of federal and state subsidies collapsed when the funding ended. In both cases, the suppliers (developers and contractors) were almost totally dependent on this market. Due to this loss of support and the inexperience of the new firms, the suppliers went bankrupt. When a critical part of the implementing coalition rests on such unstable financial ground, implementation is problematic.

Even when suppliers are readily available, the linkage forged between adopter and supplier may not be strong. This linkage is especially dependent on the role of the federal government. Some of the supplier problems in the cases occurred in federally funded demonstration projects. In Rochester, the transit authority decided to experiment with many small bus designs and contracted with seven manufacturers to build various models. Ultimately, this led to maintenance problems, as the equipment was not standard for all the small buses; and the maintenance problems, in turn, impacted on the dial-a-bus service. Because the adoption took place mostly under federal auspices, local commitment was not strong, and implementation was certainly taking place with demonstration money. This meant that the supplier problems which resulted in implementing the demonstration did not receive the attention they deserved. In the Rochester case, in particular, severe public relations problems ensued.

In the Syracuse shredder case, the terms of the demonstration grant specified that a particular shredder manufactured by a specific company, Eidal, be adopted. The federal government was interested in determining the usefulness of that particular experimental design. Unfortunately, the shredder subsequently developed severe operating problems; these mechanical difficulties may yet cause the demise of this innovation. Were it not for the lure of federal funds, local officials probably would have taken more pains in establishing a closer relationship with the supplier to ensure the adoption of a known quantity.

Availability and reliability of suppliers are not always the problem. With OPTICOM, a different kind of dilemma emerged. There was no lack of interest on the part of manufacturers. Competition was keen, as two companies bid for a large-scale contract. The firm that was selected bid slightly higher than did the loser, and the loser took the city of Syracuse to court. This caused a long delay in fully implementing an innovation that had been adopted by the agency and political leaders of Syracuse.

Finally, a somewhat different problem can occur in a rapidly emerging field where there are a number of manufacturers vying to enter the market. The difficulty is one of evaluating the credibility of alternative suppliers. This happened in the Rochester resource recovery case. After years of internal discussion and consultation with outside engineers, Monroe County officials were able to approve the specifications they desired for a resource recovery facility. The stakes for competing suppliers were high, with a potential contract of about $50 million. Four firms submitted bids. Each had recently entered the resource recovery field. They represented widely varying sectors, including military/aerospace, packaging, and traditional waste management. None had ever built a full-scale facility. Local officials, therefore, had difficulty adopting criteria by which to judge the suppliers. The solution was to have three local groups—county officials, consulting engineers, and a citizens' advisory committee—separately and independently evaluate the bids. As it happened, all three groups arrived at the same conclusion. But what if they had not?

Clients

Clients represent the third group of key actors upon whom successful implementation depends.[41] By clients, we refer to the people outside an agency who are served by a particular public service. They may be specific individuals or groups of individuals such as the elderly and handicapped in the Syracuse dial-a-bus case. They may be aggregates as large as all of the people in a particular jurisdiction such as the general public that is served by fire and police departments. They may even be people in several jurisdictions such as those served by regional authorities.

Client support may be essential to implementation, as in dial-a-bus; or it may be tangential, as in UFIRS. Generally, clients tend to be more conscious of the quality of the service than how it is delivered. There are times, however, when the "how" is perceived to be part of what is wrong. In education, the quality of teaching may be hard to discern, and clients may very well focus on the more visible techniques. Moreover, in the Syracuse education case involving school violence, it is doubtful that any technological solution would have satisfied most parents. They wanted the physical presence of policemen: a highly conventional technology in an unconventional setting.

In the computerized assessment case, the conventional technology was human judgment, a judgment that many newcomers to the town of Manlius believed to be biased in favor of established residents, if not a local power elite. Hence, reformers focused on computers as a way of providing equity in this local service. Naturally, the opposition stated that the computer would be just as unfair and would create assessment levels that would be too high. They protested and complained. It took a demonstration of the technology plus considerable persuasion to mollify them. In this case, the technology became a real issue in client relations.

Frequently, innovating agencies must acquire the favor of interest groups purporting to speak for clients (e.g., ACCORD, which represented the elderly in the dial-a-bus case in Syracuse). When these client oriented interest groups are public agencies, special dilemmas are placed before implementing agencies. In fragmented local political systems, there are many public agencies that can claim that they speak for client interests with regard to new technology. In SOVENT, for example, the Onondaga County Health Department felt obliged to protect public health standards and came close to taking UDC to court to make sure that SOVENT met local standards.

Implementing entrepreneurs will be concerned about the number of entities claiming to speak for their clients. The Syracuse fire chief, who played a large role in the early implementation phase of mini-pumpers, found that the insurance industry was concerned for the fire safety of the citizens of the city. Unless the fire insurance companies could be convinced that the mini-pumper was not detracting from the fire department's capacity to deliver a service, they were prepared to raise the insurance rates on property in the city. This would have caused much protest, effectively precluding the introduction of the mini-pumper.

Some clients press their claims on the implementers; others are constituencies whose allegiance must be won, as the Rochester Transit Authority discovered. Client organizations vary tremendously in size, power, and legitimacy. The most significant, in terms of ability to influence the course of implementation, are those organizations that are themselves political jurisdictions. Regional transit authorities and county-wide solid waste organizations must cope with clients of this kind, among others. In the case of resource recovery in Rochester, the relevant clients included the local utility company, Rochester Gas and Electric Company, a major user of the end product. This organization made the project viable by promising access to its boilers for the use of the experimental, refuse-derived fuel. Clients that provided refuse were the city of Rochester, towns, and private haulers. It is in being used by and useful to such clients that resource recovery implementers will succeed or fail in accomplishing their tasks. Indeed, the Onondaga County Solid Waste Disposal Authority may well be terminated or be radically reorganized because it has failed to secure strong linkages with the necessary clients. When the clients are cities and towns that fundamentally disagree on a given innovation, something has to give. In the Syracuse resource recovery case, this dissension was so prolonged and irreconcilable that the innovation was never adopted, and Carrier Corporation, which was to have supplied the technology, decided to withdraw from the resource recovery field.

Strategies

To establish relations with employees, suppliers, and clients that facilitate rather than impede implementation, administrative entrepreneurs have employed a number of strategies. Many are merely extensions of the strategies used in obtaining adoption decisions such as using the media. When a broad base of community support is needed, a favorable media image is sought at the outset of implementation. For example, during its first month of operation, the Syracuse Crime Control Team was featured in fifteen stories, including four editorials, published in local newspapers. In addition, there were nine television news stories. Virtually all of the media coverage favorably portrayed the experiment and helped build momentum toward incorporation. Likewise, the director of the transit authority in Syracuse has continued to cooperate with news reporters in the belief that publicity about his programs, as well as paid advertising, will increase dial-a-bus ridership.

Reassurance

Probably the most widely used technique aimed at employees is that of reassurance. Proponents carefully do whatever is necessary to allay fears on the part of groups whose support is regarded as essential to utilization. In introducing fire innovations in Syracuse, the fire chief made it clear that the new technology would not mean a loss of jobs. Indeed, even with the new technology, the Syracuse Fire Department needed additional firefighters to meet the requirements of the state-mandated 40-hour work week. Further, the fire chief made it clear that any future reduction in personnel made possible by new technologies would come through attrition, and that older firefighters would not be forced to learn new techniques. Innovations were introduced selectively to the fire companies with the largest contingent of young firefighters. In Rochester, however, there was not a strategy of reassurance. The purpose of implementing the mini-pumper was to increase productivity, based on labor savings. The mini-pumper decreased staffing requirements by twelve positions. The cost savings in manpower were estimated to be $300,000 yearly, out of a departmental budget of about $18 million. Although the mini-pumper was accepted in Syracuse, it brought such a strong reaction from the firefighters' union in Rochester that deployment of more mini-pumpers will be hotly contested there.

Reassurance was also a factor in the Rochester and Syracuse

team policing cases. Police officers in Syracuse who saw CCT as eroding their status and authority were reassured somewhat by the appointment of a "top cop" to head the crime control unit. This person was highly regarded by his peers. He was an insider who could give credibility to the rhetoric of reassurance. Thus, his internal leadership capacities were helpful in counteracting the negative effect on recruitment to CCT that resistance in the ranks had created. In Rochester, the implementing entrepreneur was equally well regarded and would, like his Syracuse counterpart, eventually become chief of police. In turn, the Rochester implementer consciously chose strong leaders to head the first CTP units. Those first leaders were able to keep morale high in their units in the early days when the units were not popular in the department.

It is clear that not only what is said and how it is said, but also who says it provides strategic reassurance. In another example, the Insurance Services Office (ISO), the chief fire insurance rating organization, apparently would not go along with the pleas of the Syracuse fire chief that the mini-pumper be given the proper certification. ISO was finally persuaded by reassurances from Public Technology, Inc., a national technical advisory organization, that intervened in the mini-pumper dispute. In another example, the implementing entrepreneur in Rochester team policing brought in the Police Foundation to reassure local elected adopters of the legitimacy of the operation.

Reassurance was also applied in client relations. In Syracuse team policing, for example, the police department management worried that the innovation might be regarded as a threat in predominantly black neighborhoods. Enlisting the help of neighborhood leaders, the police sponsored mass meetings in the neighborhoods to reassure residents that the innovation was not targeted specifically at blacks. Individual police officers in the affected neighborhoods were also encouraged to attend the regular meetings of neighborhood organizations.

In Rochester, the fire chief became alarmed when the firefighters' union conducted a campaign against implementing the mini-pumper. Union activities included distributing leaflets in the neighborhood where the mini-pumper was to be located, and city hall began to receive queries from residents who were worried about fire protection. The fire chief responded by accepting a union challenge to debate the issue in public. The unprecedented debate helped to calm neighborhood fears, and the department followed up by sending the new mini-pumper to neighborhood meetings where its use could be demonstrated and explained.

Reassurance was also used in the computerized assessment case. Not only were public hearings held to carefully explain the new system's operation, but assessment officials also demonstrated the impact of the innovation. They mailed estimates of what individual assessments would be for the following year to homeowners. An assessment hot-line was also established for the convenience of citizens who had questions about their taxes. As a vehicle for reassurance, few means are as helpful as a practical and successful demonstration that impacts directly on the individual.

Appealing Outside

Where words, actions, and demonstrations by prestigious individuals or organizations fail to secure the needed coalition for implementation, other pressures can sometimes help. This is especially true where there are potential financial rewards or penalties involved. Outside pressures can have the impact of bringing key participants together for utilization of new technology. They serve what is, in effect, a broker function. Ideally, brokers have leverage; they have "carrots to give" or "sticks to wield."[42] Skillful use of discretionary funding or regulations can help bring an implementation together.

The elderly and handicapped had their disagreements with the transit authority about the use of the Syracuse dial-a-bus, but clients and agency united in the presence of federal and state officials who had the money for expanding the system. In the Rochester dial-a-bus case, outside money has bought time for transit entrepreneurs to attempt to aggregate a coalition for innovation. The system has been implanted via federal demonstration, but a viable political base has not yet taken hold. Transit entrepreneurs, therefore, appealed for and received an extension of demonstration support beyond the initial period, in order for them to build the local coalition that they probably should have made at the outset.

In contrast to dial-a-bus, Rochester team policing entrepreneurs received outside money only after the innovation had already been implemented on a limited basis. The Police Foundation helped to expand the program. After the concept had been established city-wide, money from the Law Enforcement Assistance Administration helped with training funds to consolidate changes that had occurred. This appears to be a situation where local implementers appealed for outside help in the middle and final stages of implementation, rather than in the first stages as in other cases. Project Unique, for example, received $4,640,000 to implement its nine program components under Office of Education Title III funding.

The field of solid waste management presents the best example of the use of regulatory power to help in implementation. For seven years, the leaders of the Onondaga County Solid Waste Disposal Authority have struggled with the difficulties of maintaining a coalition of clients that is essential to making the use of the expensive shredders a viable activity. SWDA has found it useful to appeal to state regulatory officials to pressure reluctant clients such as the neighboring towns to use the shredders rather than town sanitary landfills. The same state pressure helped to convince suburban officials to support the steam station. In Rochester, resource recovery entrepreneurs obtained a commitment of $18.5 million from the New York State Department of Environmental Conservation under the 1972 Environmental Quality Bond Act. The project was inherently interjurisdictional in the sense that a number of local governments had to ally in order to make the resource recovery system viable. Outside money was a catalyst for establishing and maintaining cooperation, and, as in Syracuse, state pressures to close landfills helped make resource recovery an attractive alternative. In resource recovery, therefore, both inducements and constraints helped point local officials in a particular direction.

Bureaucratic implementers sometimes appeal for outside support even if funding or regulations are not involved. As previously mentioned, the Syracuse fire chief enlisted the support of Public Technology, Inc., to persuade the Insurance Services Office to recognize the usefulness of the mini-pumper. He also appealed for help to the New York State Department of Transportation when a competing firm challenged in court the award of the OPTICOM contract. The state testified to the legality of the use of OPTICOM under state transportation regulations, and the award was upheld. In another example, the Urban Development Corporation officials enlisted the endorsement of SOVENT by the National Bureau of Standards in order to bolster their claim that SOVENT was workable.

Too much dependence on outside support for implementation, however, can be a handicap; it can provide a false sense of security, as perhaps was true in the Rochester dial-a-bus case. Outside funding is no substitute for a local political base of support. Once federal and UDC support dried up, industrialized housing in Rochester and Syracuse proved a short-lived phenomenon. There were no local funding alternatives to take their place.

Dampening (Under-Innovating)

The period of implementation may be seen as one in which technical, administrative, and political obstacles are removed in order to progress toward full routinization (routine incorporation) of an innovation. This requires building a coalition of support among key participants in the agency's environment. Appeal to outside pressures may be regarded as an extreme implementation strategy that is used only when absolutely essential. Reassurance, however, may not be enough to mitigate local resistance. In the process of moving from the period of initial implementation to that of routinization, it may be necessary to eliminate some of an innovation's more controversial features. This strategy is called "dampening" or "under-innovating."[43] An implementing entrepreneur may decide that it is better to have a limited innovation than none at all. He frequently must strike a balance between what he wishes to accomplish and what the clients and the broader community are willing to accept.

This is brought out most strikingly in the transition of a

project from a federally funded demonstration to a locally managed effort. Invariably, the innovation is reshaped as those in charge of its implementation change. This occurred in the Syracuse CCT, the Rochester and Syracuse dial-a-bus cases, and Project Unique. Federal demonstrators want to use local sites to test and show experimental technologies that have national significance. Federal demonstrators seek to emphasize innovative features, as shown in the Rochester dial-a-bus case. Local people, especially legislators, tend to be more concerned with problem solving than innovating and have a different point of view, less favorable to innovation per se. They are increasingly sensitive to what an innovation will cost them when it becomes incorporated, and they want a technology that suits their local interests rather than one that serves the federal purposes of a national demonstration project.

Also a factor in the dampening process is the technological reality of available suppliers for the innovation. Innovations often require special hardware equipment. Finding a supplier willing to design and manufacture innovative equipment can be difficult. Manufacturers are faced with an element of risk when they specialize in this manner, especially when the product is not entirely financed locally but is partially dependent upon federal and/or state funding. Often, a highly sophisticated, government financed hardware innovation is beyond the financial ability of the locality once government funding is withdrawn.[44] In some cases, the innovation is modifed to fit the local budget and becomes incorporated. In other cases, it fails to become incorporated. Therefore, the supplier must be prepared to take the risk that an innovation may not be routinized and the venture will terminate with the demonstration phase.

The dampening strategy involves reshaping, or adapting, federally funded demonstrations promoted by Washington. When a locality deliberately chooses to dampen a federally sponsored innovation by modification, federal officials and manufacturers may consider that local officials are uninnovative. They fail to realize that the dampening strategy may be not only one of necessity but also one of practicality. That which is technically "sweet" federally may not be palatable locally.

Conclusion

The implementation process, as it applies to urban innovation, has been discussed. As has been shown, the problems are different but no less difficult at this phase of the innovation process than they were at earlier stages. The next challenge for the entrepreneur, usually at this stage an administrator a few ranks below the top official, is to complete the coalition begun during adoption. The support of the political people must be maintained, and the support of those necessary to carrying out the project must be won. Employees, clients, and suppliers become critical to successfully steering an innovation through implementation.

In the course of filling out the coalition, the implementing entrepreneur employs many strategies, some of which are unique to the implementation phase. As implementation moves from experiment and trial to routinization, dampening may become a deliberate strategy on the part of the entrepreneur. Under most circumstances, the entrepreneurial style of the zealot is not suitable for an implementer. Zealots are generally better at getting innovations underway than seeing them through.[45] Hence, the implementing entrepreneur must generally be an advocate with a clear sense of what is possible. He works day-to-day, making the necessary accommodations he hopes will permit the innovation to proceed. It is not a glamorous task, but it is absolutely essential, and the political capacity of the entrepreneur in this phase is as important as that in preadoption and adoption.

8

Incorporating Urban Innovation

Is incorporation a separate stage from implementation?[46] We believe so, although it may not be possible to identify the exact point at which incorporation begins. In our view, the Syracuse and Rochester experiences illuminate some of the more significant aspects of incorporation.

For a period of time after implementation, new urban technologies are held up to close scrutiny. They are reviewed by the agency head and watched by elected officials to see if the performance gap originally noticed has been filled. Elected officials also want to know if public tax revenues are being spent wisely; where political parties are highly competitive, these officials are sensitive to possible campaign issues. Finally, clientele groups will notice if the service has been improved. For innovations that pass muster, there are decisions to incorporate them, presumably for indefinite use. These innovations then become routinized and are considered to be a regular part of city operations. In this sense, an innovative process may be said to be "complete" at that point—a new technology has been introduced to an urban public service.

Decisions to incorporate innovations may take place at widely varying periods after they have been adopted. Implementation may be seen as an opportunity for innovations to reveal their worth and gain adherents. It may likewise be seen as a test to discover if technologies can acquire the necessary allies to survive and reach incorporation. The test can be rigorous or easy, depending upon the visibility that a technology has and the political heat that it generates. Some innovations require much adaptation, and it may be many years before they are accepted and incorporated. For others, the changes required (whether institutional, managerial, or hardware) are virtually imperceptible, and decisions are made quickly.

Aside from the controversy inherent in some innovations such as Campus Plan, as contrasted with others where there is little or no opposition such as UFIRS, there seem to be two main reasons for variations in the time needed to make a decision regarding continuation.

One reason lies in the willingness of federal officials to extend demonstrations. If federal agencies are determined that an innovation should be a showcase for the nation and that it should succeed, they will continue to fund the project, including any reorientations in, or even dampening of, the project that may be necessary to assure sufficient local support. This may well indicate that federal officials are cognizant that some technologies may take longer than others to gain local acceptance. UMTA appears to have been willing to extend the Rochester dial-a-bus demonstration to give the newly appointed transit chief, a former UMTA official, an opportunity to build a political base for the technology, which his predecessor had neglected to do.

Ordinarily, however, federal demonstrations move in and out so quickly that localities are not ready for the critical decision to use local money for operating and maintaining a technology, a benchmark of the incorporation process. In some instances, local operating budgets still include federal subsidies. This is the case in urban mass transit, but, even here, the degree of local contribution is larger than in the experimental demonstration phase. The point is that the length of federal demonstrations impacts on incorporation processes, or the probability of incorporation. The longer the demonstration, the more willing federal officials are to permit local adaptations and the more opportunity local entrepreneurs have to build, adjust, and solidify coalitions.

The other reason is that the time needed to make long-lasting decisions to continue an innovation depends upon the mix of operating and capital costs in a project. Programs that require large annual operating expenditures can be expected to have more difficulty being incorporated than those in which the capital expenditures dominate the total cost of the program. This is related also to the reversibility of the technology. Mini-pumpers, OPTICOM, shredders, resource recovery, and cable TV cannot be easily sold or otherwise abandoned. The tangible quality of hardware innovations adds visibility to sunk costs. Not incorporating such an innovation is to risk the responsibility for a "white elephant." Thus, the pressure at the local level is toward incorporating large capital projects.

Programmatic innovations are much easier to terminate since there is less tangible evidence of decision-making "mistakes." Also, in a multiprogram innovation such as Project Unique, some programs can be killed in order to protect the core of the innovation against opposition.

This is not to say that the concept of routinization has less meaning in those cases featuring hardware innovations. First, if opposition to innovations in process builds up, they may be discontinued at the first opportunity, such as a breakdown. This seems to be a possibility for the future in the case of the shredders.

Second, lack of diffusion, when diffusion was expected locally, can be understood as a failure to routinize. Thus, while SOVENT and innovative housing projects are an accomplished fact, these technologies will not be tried again soon. Only one mini-pumper has been bought in Rochester, and the union is determined to limit incorporation to that one. Rapid Water has been incorporated in Syracuse, but it is seldom used because of increases in cost. Clearly, the line between incorporation and nonincorporation is vague. "Routinization" to one person may be "nonincorporation" to another. Incorporation actually has at least two variations; incorporated innovations can be said to be arrested or continuing.

An arrested incorporation reflects a lack of support for an innovation after it is in place and has been used. Due to its nature, for example, buildings, it cannot be eliminated easily. However, because of institutional problems or better alternative technologies, including conventional technologies, there are no further efforts to deploy the technology beyond the initial order. Continuing incorporation, on the other hand, reflects satisfaction and a desire to sustain. A given system is maintained and, where necessary, replaced. Additional orders are placed when needed. In arrested incorporation, the coalition has fallen apart or has been significantly weakened relative to opposition—opposition perhaps not present throughout the previous stages of the innovation process. In continuing incorporation, the coalition has been maintained and constitutes a standing alliance around the innovation.

What is necessary to prevent either the modification or the termination of a technological change that was adopted and implemented? How do innovations become part of standard operating procedures? Three explanations come to mind: (1) successful innovations have homes in agencies that have been able to end dependence on elements external to the local jurisdiction while innovations still on trial do not; (2) successful innovations have demonstrated their usefulness on a continuing basis to all members of the adopting and implementing coalitions while innovations on trial have not; and (3) successful innovations have escaped the battlefields of urban politics while innovations on trial have not.

Ending Dependencies External to the Local Jurisdiction

Incorporation requires a locality to decide that a technology is needed. The user must be committed to the innovation. For example, neither Syracuse nor Rochester is committed to innovative housing as a technology; hence, the incorporation of such housing in the two cities must be viewed as arrested. Full commitment will result in full incorporation when localities view a new technology as so essential that if federal and state money cannot pay for it local money will. Therefore, the more a technology becomes a part of routine local financing, the more clearly it can be said to have been incorporated.

It is conceivable that the shredders, which represented a huge capital expenditure, could fall into disuse because their prime client, the city of Syracuse, is still not convinced of the merits of solid waste shredding and could abandon its support if less expensive and environmentally approved methods are discovered for solid waste disposal. Under existing financial procedures, the federal government subsidizes transit operating expenditures in the urban mass transit function, and the state and county must match this funding on a percentage basis. If the county cuts back, the federal government will do so, too, thus reducing funds for all transit services. Dial-a-bus, as a relatively new program, will be vulnerable until the local authority specifically takes money from established technologies to support the innovation. If it does so, the local authority thus signals an intention to incorporate, indicating that this technology is necessary even if other technologies must suffer.

A technology is thus always dependent upon a number of elements in its environment. However, to be incorporated, dependency at the local level is especially important. Moreover, the local dependency relationship must be reciprocal—the local users must feel dependent upon the technology. They must believe that they need it and cannot do without it. For example, once HUD subsidies were curtailed, the Syracuse and Rochester housing market could no longer support modular housing. SOVENT will not succeed in going beyond the very limited incorporation it now has attained, in part because it is dependent upon the approval of local building code officials who are now opposed to it. In contrast, innovations that have been fully incorporated are those that are least dependent upon external funding and most dependent upon local support— support which they do have. Indeed, fully incorporated innovations are so accepted that the notion of abandonment does not come up. User agencies, their clients, and the local political forces no longer give them special consideration. They are relatively autonomous and are left alone.

Demonstration of Usefulness

A primary reason for the incorporation of innovations in Syracuse and Rochester is that no one questions the usefulness of the innovations. This can be interpreted as either an overwhelming conviction on the part of coalition members concerning the merits of the innovation or, alternatively, the absence of opposition. Some innovations are incorporated because a few supportive persons are intensely interested and everyone else is indifferent. Usefulness is a subjective criterion. Adopters and implementers may differ on their views of the usefulness of an innovation. Politicians have electoral stakes; administrators have bureaucratic stakes. Suppliers want money; clients want services. If an innovation has something for each of these constituencies and, particularly, if it can continue to provide such rewards, it will be self-sustaining in the sense that the coalition will have a continuing interest in maintaining the technology.

Escaping Partisan Politics

Incorporated innovations have escaped the battlefields of urban politics. In effect, they no longer even receive the attention of elected politicians. Many urban researchers would automatically look to elected officials for the answers to the issues discussed in this study. However, our research has demonstrated that under most circumstances bureaucrats, not elected officials, dominate public policy where technological change in cities is concerned. This does not mean that there is a bureaucratic determinism, any more than that there is a technological determinism. Politicians authorize new agencies, fund them, investigate them, and reorganize them. However, where technological choice is at issue, politicians usually react to the initiatives of the bureaucrats.

Hence, technological innovation in a city depends primarily on bureaucratic rather than partisan politics. Indeed, in none of the cases that we studied was the innovation a partisan issue in a major election. The Republican opponent to Syracuse Mayor Lee Alexander attempted to make resource recovery an issue in the 1977 mayoral election. He contended that, if he were mayor, he would join with the county executive in bringing this new technology to Syracuse, whereas Alexander, by indifference, had helped bring about the defeat of resource recovery. This charge, however, failed to become an issue. The failure may have been due to the particular candidates involved, but it probably had more to do with the lack of salience that the issue had for most citizens. It suggests why so many technological choices, even those of great importance to local government, are creatures of bureaucratic rather than partisan politics. In Syracuse and Rochester, as in many other localities, partisan politics is dominated more by personalities than by issues.

As a result, changes in local party control do not necessarily place recent innovations in peril. In 1969, with the election of the first Democratic mayor and the first Democratically controlled common council in decades, Syracuse sustained a truly major shift in electoral politics. At that time, all but five of the fourteen Syracuse cases were at some stage in the decision-making process. One might expect that the change of administration would have heavily influenced the remaining nine cases. However, in only three cases (shredders, modular housing, and team policing) was there a substantial impact caused by the new officials. The new administration reversed the implied promise of the previous administration to adopt shredding and delayed the eventual decision for over a year. The new administration also reversed a decision by the previous administration to adopt modular housing. Two years later, a state agency ultimately adopted modular housing. Finally, team policing was altered, in part because the new mayor and the new police chief were fearful that a seemingly radical change in police services could not be sustained by a new administration with a weak electoral base.[47] Thus, some of the more innovative aspects of team policing were cut. In this case, dampening was the price of the innovation's survival, and the dampening was related, at least in part, to the problems of the new administration. The change of administrations impacted on technological change by interrupting a bureaucratic momentum. Politicians reacted to initiatives from a bureaucracy-centered technological process rather than vice-versa.

As in Syracuse, the Rochester innovations did not become political issues in a partisan sense, although a few reached the political issue level for some elected officials at certain points during the process of innovation. Resource recovery has been a political issue due to its cost rather than service-related issues. The same is true for dial-a-bus, which has waxed or waned over time as a political issue in both cities. Arguments may be made about the technology, but usually the problem comes down to the matter of who pays and how much. If elected officials can be satisfied on the financial question, or be persuaded that there is sufficient support within the user agency and clientele for the innovation, they may accept innovation as worth the cost in relation to other priorities and remain in the coalition which was generated from the administrative level.

Bureaucratic coalition politics requires cooperation and limitation of conflict. These are the essential ingredients of entrepreneurship and coalition building. A bureaucratic entrepreneur's capacity to aggregate acceptance can overwhelm opposition and thus contain an issue at the bureaucratic rather than the political level. As the innovation routinizes, it becomes less and less a matter of contention. Ultimately, it ceases to be an issue in any political sense; it is forgotten, accepted, and becomes part of the routine. It is off the agenda of political awareness on the part of virtually everyone. Even the bureaucrats tend not to think of it as an administrative issue at all. It has a lower priority in administrative behavior and is relegated to technicians as a technical matter. Technicians neither make nor implement policy. They "tinker" with policy, making an adjustment here and there. Their task is to maintain what is established, not to introduce something new. When this point is reached, the entrepreneur has left the scene. And why not—he is no longer needed. His very success has made his role expendable.

Conclusion

The goal of urban innovation is routine utilization. Ideally, adoption and implementation lead to the routine use of a new technology. This goal is not reached automatically. No magic, no technological imperative, and no unseen hand make the use of new technology inevitable. To the contrary, this study reveals the difficulties in innovating. Someone at the local level must *want* to innovate and to tend to the politics of the process. This requires coalitions.

Coalition building is needed to get an innovation to the verge of incorporation. Coalition stabilizing is what it takes to complete the process. When the alliance is in equilibrium, it ceases to require a conscious effort by an entrepreneur to keep it going; it becomes self-sustaining. We can say that the technology has achieved the political conditions for incorporation. The technology is a necessary part of the bureaucracy and its constituency.

Those who join the organization after the innovation is incorporated are trained or socialized into the techniques that are now routine. For new police officers in Syracuse and Rochester, team policing is normal, not novel. For a recent recruit to the Syracuse Fire Department, work without the mini-pumper is unthinkable.

However, incorporation implies even more. The bureaucracy is surrounded by a network of constituents, political sovereigns, and other organizations that take a technology's continuation for granted. Try to take away dial-a-bus from Syracuse, for example, and the elderly and handicapped will protest. They depend on the technology, and the Syracuse mass transit system authority has come to depend on them for political support. The technology has become central to the overall relationship between bureaucracy and its political environment. An infrastructure and support system has institutionalized the innovation. An incorporated innovation then becomes extremely difficult to dislodge. Many barriers to innovation were once innovations themselves.

So it is with all innovations that go the full cycle. In the Rochester resource recovery case, a large-scale innovation has been adopted, and initial implementation is underway. A new bureau has been created to manage the completion and routine operation of this facility. Its capacity to maintain the coalition that the earlier entrepreneurs helped to create will determine how quickly or whether the technology routinizes. As the Syracuse shredder case exemplifies, coalitions do fall apart even where technologies with large hardware costs are involved. A favorable political environment for technological change has to be nurtured, usually over a long period of time. Either the bureaucracy becomes the center of a viable local coalition, or the innovation will be terminated once external supports are withdrawn.

9
Conclusions

Political coalitions are critical to incorporated innovations. Local entrepreneurs, primarily bureaucrats, are key forces in creating such coalitions. What factors make for successful entrepreneurs, stable coalitions, and, thus, complete innovations? What implications do these findings have for federal policy efforts to facilitate technology transfer to cities? To answer these questions, we must examine our cases from the standpoint of outcomes and try to relate how characteristics of the innovation, the organization, and the environment in which they interact affect the chances for bureaucratic entrepreneurs to arise and form winning coalitions.

The Outcomes

The cases yield a variety of outcomes. Of the twenty innovation attempts we studied, few fully succeeded. Most fell short of the original objectives of their sponsors. Some fell far short, and those that fell the shortest were those that were rejected at the point of adoption. In this category were Campus Plan, Syracuse resource recovery, and three elements of the multifaceted Rochester Project Unique.

The other cases were innovations that moved beyond adoption to varying degrees. Exactly where the dial-a-bus in Rochester stands is subject to some debate. There were local resources involved, but this was essentially a federal demonstration project. Implementation has largely taken place under federal auspices. If federal money were removed, the probability is that dial-a-bus in Rochester would be terminated. Dial-a-bus is one of those instances where federal funding masks the weakness of the coalition of support undergirding adoption and use. The other innovations which are in the implementation stage are computerized assessment, cable TV, and Rochester resource recovery. The prognosis for incorporation of the first two is fairly good, although cable TV is just starting to be implemented.

While many of our cases did reach incorporation, a number of these are less than complete successes. Thus, Syracuse dial-a-bus is well regarded locally, but it is constrained by the general financial problems of the transit authority. The housing cases in both cities constitute arrested incorporations, since there is little inclination at the local level to acquire additional versions of these innovations. Similarly, the Rochester Fire Department has stopped further acquisition of mini-pumpers. The Syracuse Police Department has only partially incorporated the team policing concept, and the fire department has acquired Rapid Water but has seldom used it. The two major elements of Project Unique have been incorporated in Rochester, and four other elements are in forms quite different from the originally contemplated innovation. Solid waste shredding is close to incorporation, but there is a considerable controversy about its future continuation. In fact, there is a chance that it will cease to be used.

What are the most successful outcomes? In Syracuse, there are the three fire innovations: UFIRS, OPTICOM, and the mini-pumper. Also, there is the police department's School Resources and Information Program. In Rochester, there are two components of Project Unique and Coordinated Team Patrol. Table 13 illustrates a summary of the continuum along which the cases fall, from adoption through incorporation, and the length of time involved. It should be understood that the table is correct as of fall 1977.

What are the factors that help explain these outcomes? Given the fact that it takes a coalition of support to get innovations adopted and used, what brings out and maintains such coalitions? Why do some coalitions fall apart? A number of variables are involved. Among the most important are those

Table 13

OUTCOMES OF CASES IN
SYRACUSE AND ROCHESTER

Case	Outcome			Approx. Duration (Years)
	Adoption	Implementation	Incorporation	
S: Campus Plan	——→			6
S: Resource Recovery	——→			3-1/2*
R: Part of Project Unique	——→			1-1/2
R: Resource Recovery	————→			7*
S: Cable TV	—————→			5*
R: Dial-a-bus	—————————→			7*
R: Industrialized Housing		————————→		5
S: Modular Housing		————————→		4
S: SOVENT		————————→		3-1/2
S: Dial-a-bus		—————————————→		6*
S: CCT		—————————————→		7
S: Rapid Water		—————————————→		2
R: Mini-pumper		—————————————→		2
R: Part of Project Unique		—————————————→		4-1/2
S: Solid Waste Shredding		—————————————→		9*
S: Computerized Assessment		—————————————→		6*
S: UFIRS			——————————————→	4
S: OPTICOM			——————————————→	8
S: Mini-pumper			——————————————→	2
S: SRIP			——————————————→	2
R: Part of Project Unique			——————————————→	9
R: CTP			——————————————→	8

(Vertical column labels: Decision to Adopt · Full Implementation · Full Incorporation)

*Active consideration of the innovation still in progress.

Key: Adopting Agency
    R=Rochester
    S=Syracuse

relating to the innovations and organizations at issue and the ways they are linked through the political process.

The Innovations

Characteristics of the innovation matter. If a technology does not work, it will not be adopted. If a technology that has been adopted operates below expectations, as in the Syracuse shredding case, it may well be abandoned. Separability helps, especially in larger-scale innovations. Campus Plan was presented as a complete package, but Project Unique was offered as a combination of programs that could be separated. Campus Plan and all that went with it were rejected at the beginning of the innovation process. Three elements of Project Unique were totally rejected at the time of adoption, but others were modified in varying degrees during implementation. Two, probably the major components of the effort, did make it through to routinization.

Technologies that are separable tend also to be incremental. They are easily understood, or at least not perceived as threatening. Thus, they are clearly advantaged. Large-scale, costly, and seemingly irreversible technologies have greater problems in being adopted and used than those that are small, cheap, and seen as easily abandoned if they fail to work. These characteristics are more important than whether the technologies are hardware or managerial. However, hardware technologies, because of their tangible quality, appear to have more appeal to decision makers than do those less easily seen or understood.

This is not to suggest that radical, costly, nonseparable, and complex technologies are inappropriate for local government. However, they may well be. We would argue that outcomes are associated with inputs, and technological inputs vary in their effects on the intervening process. Thus, some technologies only require small, easily-assembled coalitions, while others demand large, complex, and unwieldy alliances often stretching across jurisdictional lines. Many large-scale technologies require intergovernmental aid to get started and be maintained. As an example, resource recovery possesses all the attributes of a technology that makes innovation in the city difficult. It is not surprising that it failed in Syracuse the first time it came up for decision. If it succeeds in Rochester, it will demonstrate that the characteristics of a technology that are negative for innovation can be overcome. Technology, after all, is only one of the inputs to the local governmental decision-making process. *Who* backs the technology and *how* it is supported are also factors that matter. They certainly have been important in bringing resource recovery in Rochester to its current point beyond the adoption decision.

There are two additional characteristics of urban technology that appear to enhance the factors that are favorable to coalition building and, thus, adoption and use. The same characteristics, if associated with hard-to-innovate technology, would serve to mitigate its disadvantageous features. These characteristics relate to improved services and cost savings.[48] The first attracts bureaucracy and its clients; the second gains the favor of elected officials and their budgetary staffs.

Table 14 presents an estimation of the cost and service efficiencies of the Syracuse and Rochester innovations. Service efficiency is a stronger predictor of decision-making outcomes than cost efficiency. If service efficiency is widely perceived as an outcome by the participants involved, the innovation has a good possibility of being incorporated. In Syracuse and Rochester, the innovations that were most fully incorporated were regarded as yielding service efficiencies. The lesson here may be that innovation is so difficult that a technology must at least be *perceived* as providing the strong expectation of improved services; otherwise, it will have practically no chance for incorporation. This can be explained by the political unacceptability of losses in service efficiency. The cases with clear gains in both cost efficiency and service efficiency were those that had positive outcomes, in the sense of reaching incorporation or of having a high probability of doing so. In situations where cost efficiency was ambiguous but gains in service efficiency were probable, the innovations were adopted and have achieved implementation in varying degrees. However, in cases where service efficiency was ambiguous, although cost efficiency was probable or ambiguous, the

Table 14

COST EFFICIENCY AND SERVICE EFFICIENCY

Service Efficiency

	Negative	Ambiguous	Probable	Clear
Cost Efficiency				
Negative		S:Campus Plan S:Shredder		
Ambiguous		S:Steam Station S:SOVENT R:Dial-a-bus R:Industri- alized Housing	S:Cable TV S:Crime Control Team R:Project Unique R:Resource Recovery	S:Rapid Water R:Coordinated Team Patrol
Probable		S:Modular Housing	S:UFIRS	S:OPTICOM S:Dial-a-bus
Clear			S:SRIP R:Mini-pumper	S:Computerized Assessment S:Mini-pumper

Negative   Questionable   Positive
Outcomes   Outcomes   Outcomes

Key: Adopting Agency
     R=Rochester
     S=Syracuse

innovations had negative outcomes: either rejection or a likelihood of not achieving incorporation.

As noted, our cases feature five relatively unambiguous successes, in the sense of full incorporation: Syracuse OPTI-COM, UFIRS, the mini-pumper, and SRIP, and Rochester Coordinated Team Patrol. Other incorporations are of a more ambiguous character. To cite two examples, Project Unique has been incorporated *in part,* and only one mini-pumper has been incorporated in Rochester. Looking at the most clear-cut successes, we find that cost efficiency was cited as an attribute of the innovation. In the one where it was not, Rochester Coordinated Team Patrol, it could not be argued that the innovation raised costs above what they would have been otherwise. It would seem that innovations promising service efficiencies can overcome cost problems, but those lacking such qualities cannot. Ideally, both kinds of attributes would be present.

Entrepreneurs who succeeded usually cited both attributes of innovations in persuading skeptics. They argued that a technology not only would improve services, but also would save money. Whether or not these contentions are true may matter less than the fact that they are believed by a winning coalition. Veracity is in the mind of the beholder, and, sometimes, perceptions depend mostly upon the capacity of an entrepreneur to make a persuasive case for the innovation. In other words, some characteristics of the technology are not inherent at all; they are the rhetoric of the entrepreneur.

The Organizations

Two kinds of organizational characteristics count in local technological innovation. The first of these is intraorganizational; the second is extraorganizational. One provides an internal support system for innovation; the other, external support. Together, they give organizations capacity to innovate.

The internal and external attributes reinforce one another. An organization with strong support systems can aspire to complex, sophisticated, and expensive technologies that one not so endowed can scarcely imagine. The ability to innovate derives from more general organizational attributes. Agencies that are powerful, both internally and externally, can usually get a variety of tasks accomplished. Those that are weak usually can do little. Innovation is naturally easier for stronger organizations than it is for weak ones.

However, innovating is a special capacity of organizations. There are many powerful entities that seldom innovate, and a number of not so formidable agencies that do a great deal, considering what they have. As technology is only part of the answer as to why innovations succeed or fail at the local level, so are organizational variables but a piece of the puzzle. There is no doubt that they are a critical piece. Match an organization lacking resources to innovate (e.g., Onondaga County Solid Waste Disposal Authority) with an innovation having attributes that promise trouble (e.g., resource recovery), and the potential for failure is very high.

Internal Support

Professionalism, leadership, high morale, and slack resources[49] are key ingredients that make for high intraorganizational capacity to innovate. One makes another possible, including the creation of slack resources. Professionalism refers to work related skills and techniques as well as to the sense of commitment to citizens with whom those skills are put to use. Professionals read journals in their field, attend professional meetings, and know the leaders in their specialty, as well as the laggards. Consequently, they are aware of performance gaps in their organizations. They listen to various business suppliers. They keep abreast of federal and state initiatives. They aggressively search for solutions and are open to ideas. Above all, professionals are service oriented. They care about the quality of service they deliver to clients. They also try to save money where possible, but not at the expense of diminished service to clients.

Such a model of professionals is, of course, an abstraction from reality. Yet, it is clear that the professional image is in the mind of many civil servants in Syracuse and Rochester, especially those in the agencies where innovation has travelled farthest. Ironically, professionalism has also led to significant battles in these two cities and thus has held up innovation. Professionals care about the techniques of delivery. Indeed, their jobs and perquisites may depend on these techniques. Hence, the introduction of a new technology into an agency may be seen by one professional group as a threat imposed upon it by another professional group. In the team policing cases, the detectives correctly perceived themselves as adversely affected by the proposed change. In the Campus Plan, some teachers perceived themselves as being injured by the innovation. In the first instance, the opponents did, in fact, lose. In the second, the opposition by some teachers was able to help defeat the innovation.

The point is that professionalism does not necessarily lead to the success of a *specific* innovation. It does, however, create a climate within organizations that is more favorable to innovation in general than is found where organizations are patronage ridden. And, when professionals agree or are brought into agreement, they become the core of a formidable organizational interest group. They constitute a pressure group endowed with governmental status.

Internal leadership helps to transform professionalism into an organizational resource for innovation. The head of the agency or someone else in an authoritative position finds ways to soften professional differences and bring cohesion to the agency. Often, leadership of this kind is best exemplified in the implementation process, where the impacts of a new technology become most apparent. In paramilitary organizations such as police and fire departments, traditions of hierarchy augment the ability of leaders to enforce their views. Such traditions (and sanctions) were apparently not available to the superintendent of schools in the Campus Plan case. Thus, organizations differ in terms of hierarchical control as a leadership tool.

The primary strategy of leaders attempting to enlist employee support in organizations was one of reassurance. This was accomplished not only by accommodating employee concerns, but also by appointing highly respected insiders to key roles in implementing the new technology.

The concern for reassurance highlights the importance of organizational morale to implementing innovations. Morale is a major intraorganizational resource that can enhance the innovation option. The Syracuse fire chief used innovation to improve the morale of his firefighters, especially the newer members of the department. While reassuring older firefighters that they would not lose their jobs, he introduced new technologies that made the younger firefighters feel better about themselves and their agency. They felt that they were getting the best equipment and were members of an innovative organization with national stature. High morale makes an organization more receptive to innovation. The process can become circular, with innovation becoming an agency's trademark.

Finally, there is the matter of slack resources. Having slack resources obviously helps in getting innovative activities underway. Since most local organizations do not have a line item in their budget for research and development, they must find money and divert personnel from ongoing projects to initiate that which is new. Again, the more successful cases revealed instances where slack resources were made available, at least at the preadoption phase. In UFIRS, existing agency resources were used to make the purchase. In SRIP, the same was true in terms of allocating personnel. In Rochester team policing, the department found the resources to move the innovation well into the implementation stage before getting slack resources from outside. In short, when organizational leaders want to innovate in a certain direction, they find a way to obtain slack resources.

The internal characteristics that make for innovation can be seen to relate to one another. Professionalism provides a base of good people with awareness and desire. High morale is a consequence of professionals directed toward goals about which they agree. Leadership includes a willingness to risk resources of money and people to get innovation underway, if only through the initial seeding of ideas. Perhaps the most important resource of all is the attention, energy, and continued enthusiasm of the leader of the organization over the time it takes for any new technology to move through the various phases. If the leaders do not give their support to the innovation process, their indifference will create a barrier to change within the agency.

External Support

Agencies vary, not only in internal (intraorganizational) resources that they bring to bear upon innovation, but also in external (extraorganizational) resources. Agencies are part of functional systems consisting of a constellation of organizations concerned with specific urban services (e.g., law enforcement, fire, solid waste, mass transit). These organizations and individuals can be a source of real strength in aiding innovation, or they can be a source of little that is positive and much that is negative from the point of view of the local organization. Opposition does not have to be active to be effective. It can consist of passive instruments such as rules, laws, zoning ordinances, insurance rates, and the lack of interest on the part of those whose support is essential.

What is the nature of the external variables or support systems?[50] To address this question, it is useful to visualize the local agency as the hub of a wheel. There are three dominant spokes, or interorganizational lines of activity: one involves federal/state relations; another concerns supplier relations; and the third is the agency's local relations.

1. *Federal/state relations.* A set of relations of ever-increasing importance to local organizations are those that extend upward, vertically, to state and federal counterparts. The relations along these vertical lines differ considerably from function to function. In some functions, intergovernmental relations are well-developed; in others, they are still being established. Some federal and state counterparts provide incentives to localities to innovate; others do not. In some functional systems, relations are strained and marked by regulatory approaches toward local government; in others, the regulatory tool is not an option.

There are few uniformities across these vertical cuts. Perhaps one is the lament by federal people concerned with innovation that local agencies are slow to adopt and use new technology. Perhaps a second is the cry from the localities that the federals do not understand their problems. Perhaps a third is from the states, which question whether Washington or the cities appreciate their pivotal role in technology transfer.

One of the more highly developed intergovernmental systems for local innovation is urban mass transit. There is a visible, relatively well-funded organization in Washington: the Urban Mass Transportation Administration (UMTA). There are reasonably strong analogs at the state level. UMTA, moreover, has innovation as part of its mission. UMTA's role can extend throughout the stages of innovation experienced by the local organization. Federal transit money can help to develop, demonstrate, and diffuse new technology. Through operating subsidies, it can subsidize the incorporation of technology.

The same cannot be said of a number of other urban functions. For example, fire does not as yet have an intergovernmental support system of any consequence. There is an agency in Washington, but it is a relatively small and peripheral activity in the Department of Commerce, a department not known for a strong interest in local fire departments. A bureaucratic entrepreneur in a local transit agency can thus expect more help from Washington than can one in a fire organization. A similar comparison might be made between law enforcement, with its relatively well developed intergovernmental support system, and resource recovery, with one that is yet emerging.

The existence or nonexistence, the quality or imperfections of these intergovernmental relations matter to local user-agencies. They affect incentives. They impact upon entre-preneurial strategies. They can be the dominant support system in the agency's environment, enhancing dramatically its capacity to innovate, or they can make little difference. Much depends upon the characteristics of the functional "spoke" in question. Much also depends upon the effects of other spokes that feed into local user agencies.

2. *Supplier relations.* A second extraorganizational dimension of the user agency is its relation with the supplier industry. Agencies are users, not sellers. What if available technology is not particularly innovative? Federal agencies may wish to foster innovation. Local organizations may need and want innovation. But these conditions, in and of themselves, do not mean that technological innovation will occur. It is the role of industry to supply technology, at least of the hardware variety, on a commercial basis. When industry is unwilling or unable to do this, there is a critical gap in the institutional network of technology transfer. Similarly, an agency's problem may be one of management. If available techniques cannot help, the agency's leadership may turn to consultants and others such as professional associations. Consultants are also suppliers of

urban technology. An agency's capacity thus depends, in part, on supplier availability.

Every local user agency has a supplier industry for which it is a potential customer. As with intergovernmental relationships, supplier-user linkages vary. The dominant impression from our work to date, however, is that most of the industries are less than innovative. Most are characterized by small firms that do little or no research and development, and their managements are uneasy about developing and marketing new technology. They are geared to marketing proven rather than novel products. At least, this appears to be the view of industry from the perspective of the user.

Some industries serving urban users are obviously stronger than others in their capacity to innovate. The resource recovery industry, which is still in a formative stage, is revolutionizing the solid waste disposal field. Many of the companies that have entered this industry are from high technology sectors. They are aggressive, forward looking, and competitive. The urban mass transit industry also includes some firms with innovative capability, particularly those that have entered urban mass transit from aerospace fields.

In most other areas, user agencies face difficulties when they look toward suppliers. Even for the resource recovery and urban mass transit agencies, finding a supplier for certain technologies can be difficult. A major part of the technological environment of the city is not especially dynamic. The absence of a vigorous, progressive supplier industry is clearly a barrier to innovation in the urban sector. However, it should be noted that just because firms are innovative does not necessarily mean they or their customers are successful. Many industrial innovators who have sought to transfer from aerospace to urban markets have failed. The point is that user capacity to innovate depends, in part, upon what technology is available. The low capacity of a supplier industry to innovate will inevitably be reflected in the aspirations of the user.

3. *Local relations.* The problems along the intergovernmental and supplier spokes of the user-agency innovation system are at least equalled by those in the user agency's local environment. The local environment has two dimensions. One

is intralocal and refers to the array of forces within a particular political jurisdiction. The other is interlocal and relates to the dimension of local governmental life that cuts across two or more jurisdictions. An example of the former is the police department compared to the other agencies in the city of Syracuse. An example of the latter is the Syracuse Police Department in relation to the county law enforcement agencies.

All agencies must cope with intralocal politics. However, some are more impacted by the interlocal variety than others. The nature of their task immerses them in interlocal politics. The urban mass transit authorities, for example, have regional responsibilities. The solid waste agencies in both areas had to deal with the county, the city, and numerous towns. The complications of decision making for a user organization in an intralocal setting are considerable enough, given the need to satisfy political officials, the public, the unions, the press, clientele, etc. They are more complex where interlocal disputes are concerned, if only because the sheer number of participants scales upward.

There is a special problem with user agencies that have interlocal responsibilities. The question of their legitimacy can be raised by local political authorities, and this affects their ability to implement their innovations. A related matter is the issue of their accountability. This is brought out in those functions that do not quite fit existing governmental divisions of responsibility, including public and private divisions as in housing.

The shredding and resource recovery cases point up the dilemmas of organizations with several municipal constituents. The agencies are administrative; the clients are political. Who is accountable to whom? The question never seemed to be resolved in the Syracuse resource recovery case, a fact that illustrates a common malady of metropolitan-wide organizations such as the Onondaga County Solid Waste Disposal Authority. The organization is large-scale and presumably a match for both the problem and the technology to be applied. However, this organization was revealed to have responsibility without requisite power. It could not play the bureaucratic entrepreneurial role. The politics were too much for it. It lost, or yielded, control of the situation to the county executive and a private sector entrepreneur, Carrier Corporation. In Rochester, the comparable organization, a bureau in the Monroe County Department of Public Works, was so underdeveloped that there was no question that leadership would have to come from the political levels. Indeed, a major part of political decision making in the Rochester resource recovery case lay in designing an organization for implementing the technology.

The difficulty is that, while many problems become interlocked, power remains fragmented and intralocal. Politics remains decentralized. New organizations do not necessarily displace older organizations. The city may transfer functions to counties and regions, but it retains the means of vetoing programs it does not like. For user agencies, the politics of the intralocal arena are familiar, while those of the interlocal setting are relatively new. Increasingly, the politics of the one interconnects with that of the other. As it does, existing user organizations are hard-pressed to make the requisite linkages. The nature of these linkages, both intra- and interlocal, are thus a major factor in the capacities of local organizations to adopt and use new technology.

The Entrepreneurs

These various characteristics of innovations, organizations, and organizational environments affect outcomes. They do so either by making it easier or more difficult for local technological entrepreneurs to arise and play their linkage role. Entrepreneurs link a public problem with an innovative solution. They build necessary coalitions among adopters, implementers, clients, and suppliers that make it possible for local public organizations to adopt and use new technology. Entrepreneurship requires a blending of technical and professional judgment and political skills.

The bureaucratic entrepreneur is especially well placed, strategically, for the linkage function. If the function already exists, as is usually the case, the innovation is perceived as a newer way of doing what the organization already does. Hence, bureaucratic entrepreneurs link organizational search and planning with the local political processes necessary to adopt, implement, and incorporate the innovation. If the function, and thus the technology, are new to the city, the political level must adopt. But it must create an innovative organization to carry out its decision; otherwise, what is adopted will not be implemented. Hence, bureaucratic entrepreneurship becomes central to innovation in the city. Therefore, the capacity of entrepreneurs to play their linkage role is an issue of prime importance to those who would further urban innovation.

The technical side of entrepreneurship requires a knowledge of problems and available solutions. It requires imagination. The entrepreneur need not be a technically trained individual, although this helps; however, it is important that he have access to technical judgment he trusts, as the police chief did with respect to the scientist in Syracuse team policing. A sense of balance seems to be essential in bureaucratic entrepreneurs. Bureaucratic personalities range from those who act as zealots to those who are effective advocates for their agencies.[51] The former singlemindedly pursue technology, sometimes at the risk of their careers, whereas the latter compromise. An entrepreneur outside the bureaucracy must, of necessity, take financial risks which can lead to loss of investment and even bankruptcy, as seen in the housing cases. The evidence suggests that cities do not need the largest, most sophisticated items available. There are so many political uncertainties associated with innovation at the local level that adding technical uncertainties can be self-defeating. In other words, entrepreneurship does require a sense of technology as a variable in decision making. By definition, the entrepreneur is an innovator, but to innovate does not require going to extremes. As seen in the Rochester dial-a-bus and Syracuse Campus Plan cases, some of our more zealous entrepreneurs promoted a solution in which discontinuity from existing methods created problems in acceptance.

Of course, the purely technical judgments cannot ever be totally separated from the purely political side of the entrepreneur's task. The entrepreneur has to link an innovation with an organization (indeed, a set of organizations and political actors) over time. The user organization is itself an environment for the innovation. Moreover, the organization exists in an environment that sets limits and provides opportunities in moving innovations forward. For example, the existence or nonexistence, the quality or imperfections of intergovernmental environments matter to local entrepreneurs. They affect incentives; they impact upon strategies. A fire chief, for example, relates more to his local environment, partly because he has no choice; at best, the intergovernmental line is weak. His innovations are likely to be relevant to the local setting, but difficult to finance. On the other hand, urban mass transit administrators, because their agency is regional and their local connections not clear-cut, may gear their planning more to intergovernmental than local needs. They have resources, but they must struggle to satisfy local clients. At the same time, in an emerging area such as resource recovery, local entrepreneurs may not know who their Washington counterpart is because of the inevitable bureaucratic jockeying for position and power between the Environmental Protection Agency, the Department of Energy, and other agencies in this new field. Thus, every local entrepreneur can see a different intergovernmental environment. What they all see and uniformly lament is the instability of the environment. What Washington wants today, it seems not to want tomorrow. Under such circumstances, many local entrepreneurs find planning difficult and innovation exasperating. Nevertheless, they do try.

It is the special role of the bureaucratic entrepreneur to adapt innovations, organizations, and coalition environments in such a way as to enhance the probability that an innovation will be accepted at the local level. Entrepreneurs link and match; in doing so, they build support. In the process, both innovations and organizations are reshaped. In UFIRS, OPTICOM, mini-pumper, SRIP, and Rochester team policing, the more successful innovations, both the organization and coalition environment were changed as the innovation was introduced, as was the technology.

Adaptation takes the form of limiting the amount of a technology acquired (e.g., the Rochester mini-pumper and Syracuse Rapid Water cases). It also includes the configuration of the innovation. In the Syracuse mini-pumper case, the user organization worked closely with the supplier in designing the vehicle. In the Syracuse dial-a-bus case, the coalition environment (particularly the elderly and handicapped) participated in the design. As the dial-a-bus was implemented, the way the technology was *used*, not just the technology, was altered to reflect coalition needs and what certain adopters would willingly finance. In most cases, adaptation during implementation is a dampening strategy. Dampening rubs some of the innovative edges off technology. If dial-a-bus in Rochester survives, it will undoubtedly be a less sophisticated and extensive system than originally contemplated or demonstrated.

The limits of bureaucratic entrepreneurship lie where problems are not matched by existing functions and organizations. Cable TV and resource recovery are examples of problems or opportunities beyond the matching capacity of existing public organizations. Technology is available, but is the "receptacle"[52] available? Need the user be a *public* organization? The decision surely will not be made by bureaucratic entrepreneurs. It will be determined by political leaders who will then make it possible (or impossible) for bureaucratic entrepreneurs to act.

In conclusion, our study indicates that there is innovation being attempted and even accomplished at the local level. Technology transfer to the city is technology transfer to urban public services. Since urban public services are dominated by core agencies charged with service delivery functions, it should not be surprising that the "who" in local innovation generally is the bureaucratic entrepreneur. Where the *service* is new to the city, however, elected officials must play the entrepreneurial role within local government.

In either situation, the fragmentation of local governmental authority requires coalition building. To build coalitions requires changes in the technology and in the city and its institutions. Since change is difficult and often resisted, the local entrepreneur invariably faces a formidable challenge. Any help that federal policy can provide the entrepreneur would undoubtedly be appreciated. But the real task lies, as always, at the local level. Unless there is the spirit and reality of entrepreneurship, a push for innovation from outside leads nowhere.

10
Implications for Federal Officials

This study focused on the process of urban technological innovation from the vantage point of local users. Because we did not extensively probe the federal role in these cases, it is difficult to make recommendations based on these particular cases. We have been exposed mostly to one viewpoint, that of local officials, on what federal officials or federal policy may have done right or wrong in influencing the local decision-making process. With that caveat in mind, however, we believe that the study does yield a number of general findings that have federal policy implications.

1. The key factor in urban government innovation is the local entrepreneur. Under most conditions, this is a bureaucratic entrepreneur. In working with the city, federal officials concerned with technology transfer would do well to ask with whom they should be working. Ordinarily, it is the bureaucratic entrepreneur, the head of a line agency. Local entrepreneurs need to be strengthened in terms of both their technical and political capacities. New training materials might well be sponsored that would create a new generation of local officials who better combine these two skills. Federal officials simply need to be more conscious of the importance of such entrepreneurs, since they are key to the great bulk of urban innovations. The discovery and development of such entrepreneurs should be a growing priority for federal officials charged with transferring new technology to the city.

2. Innovations that reach incorporation are those that represent locally initiated efforts in response to problems

and/or opportunities perceived locally by line agency officials, elected and appointed policymakers, and clientele groups. The principal institutional mechanism that needs to be identified to ensure adoption, implementation, and incorporation is a strong, locally-based, bureaucracy-centered coalition. It follows that federal technology transfer policy makers should work toward helping bureaucratic and other entrepreneurs build professionally competent agencies. These agencies should be supported at the local level by additional expertise, politicians, and a continuing clientele market for the service provided by the innovation. What must be developed is a bureaucracy surrounded by a pressure system geared toward obtaining and then maintaining an innovation.

One way that federal officials can help to build such coalitions is by carefully considering what types of federal aid are to be extended to localities. There is a need for federal funding that is both categorical and general. Federal funding (which creates slack resources) will be of greater help to bureaucratic entrepreneurs if it is categorical. Such funds work through channels of strength of functional agencies and, thus, become a part of the agency's general support system. Broader-based grants work to benefit central executives. Innovations that do not fit existing functions or centers of bureaucratic strength require entrepreneurship at the legislative or chief executive level.

What we are arguing is not only that federal officials become actively involved in promoting such coalitions but, at the very least, that they should also be increasingly aware that the primary barriers to innovation at the local level are multiple, complex, and interconnected. They must think about the user-agency in the context of its internal and external support systems. By strengthening such support systems (agency capacity, federal programs, supplier industry, interlocal and intralocal relations), they can work to build an infrastructure for urban innovation.

3. Federal technology transfer policy makers must also take a broader and longer-range view of their role.[53] They must think not only about innovation, but about innovation processes; not only about adoption, but about implementation

and incorporation. They should ask *what* and *who* it takes to obtain incorporation and try to get the necessary actors in concert as early as possible in support of an innovation. This is forward planning that begins with what is wanted at the end—incorporation.

4. Federal officials ought to be aware of the important role that state government plays in the urban technological innovation process.[54] Our study found this state government role to be critical. Although the state often supplemented federal funding, the most influential state intervention was the enactment of laws and regulations. Local governments are creatures of their respective state governments. In our cases in New York State, state laws or regulations initiated or guided local decision-making processes that led to innovation in ten of the twenty Syracuse-Rochester cases. In some respects, this type of intervention, which is not always *intended* to induce local innovation, is a more efficient stimulant of innovation and is more beneficial to local agencies than are federal interventions. Local officials pay closer attention to laws and regulations than they do to discretionary federal assistance. Laws and regulations also stimulate agencies to build capacity from within for a sustained effort to accomplish innovation.

Thus, state action can be a powerful complementary force to federal action in promoting local innovations. Federal officials would do well to explore the ways that their *inducements* to innovation can be "piggybacked" with state *constraints* which trigger the local decision-making process. Ideally, a single agency should have the ability to offer both inducements and constraints. But since this is rarely the case at federal mission agencies, federal officials need to look to the states for assistance. A recent example of this approach can be found in the Resource Conservation and Recovery Act of 1976, which offers fiscal inducements to state governments to bring local solid waste disposal practices under stricter regulations.

5. Finally, in considering whether and how to encourage local technological innovation, federal officials should not lose sight of the complexity of political relations among local, proximate jurisdictions. In only five of the twenty cases were local agencies able to adopt an innovation without the

assistance, cooperation, or permission of agencies or units of government in neighboring jurisdictions. Local regulatory control, lack of clear jurisdiction over a service area, or dependence on a neighboring jurisdiction's help can stop an innovation, as in the Campus Plan and resource recovery cases in Syracuse. Such conditions are part of the local climate for change which federal officials should investigate before proceeding.[55]

Another of the "givens" in the local climate that should not be overlooked is the attitude of local elected officials, especially the chief executive (mayor, city or county manager, county executive, etc.). In Syracuse and Rochester, the chief executive rarely took an active role in the innovation process. The exceptions were the cases in which the policy problem and proposed innovation did not fit the function of an existing local bureaucratic agency. However, this should not imply that potential did not exist for an active role by the chief executive.

In Syracuse and Rochester, the chief executive influenced innovation primarily by appointing independent, highly professional line agency heads and allowing those bureaucratic officials a great deal of discretion. In other localities, however, this might not be the case. Chief executives vary in the degree to which they oversee the operation of their line agencies, including decisions to innovate.[56] They can promote or hinder the innovation process. Federal officials, therefore, ought to be familiar with the role of local chief executives, their attitudes toward innovations, and their linkage with the bureaucracy-centered coalition.

Specific Federal Intervention Strategies

Aside from these general prescriptions, federal officials can learn from the experience of specific federal intervention strategies as they were applied in the Syracuse and Rochester cases. The presence of the federal government was felt in all but one of the twenty cases (computerized assessment). Some patterns of federal involvement were clearly more effective than others.[57] What are the circumstances for appropriate federal intervention, and what strategies are best?

Federal Funding

Federal funding occurred in eleven of the twenty cases. The lesson to be learned from this is that some types of funding stimulate innovation more than others. In our cases, there were two general types of federal funding: planning grants and various kinds of capital and operating grants.

Planning grants are very effective if they help local entrepreneurs put together a coalition. This occurred in the Project Unique and Syracuse dial-a-bus cases. Federal agencies should take precautions so that planning funds help form rather than prevent critical linkages with clientele groups. In Campus Plan, planning funds were spent almost entirely in-house, and an opportunity for stimulating a coalition was lost. That was a fatal mistake.

In ten cases, federal funding took the form of capital and operating grants and subsidies. Without any doubt, federal funding of this nature is a *sine qua non* for certain types of urban innovation. Project Unique, the three housing cases, the Crime Control Team and the two dial-a-bus operations could not have occurred without significant intergovernmental transfers. Even so, there are a number of lessons in the Syracuse and Rochester experience.

1. Grants need not be large to be effective. Small-scale demonstrations can lead to local commitment to underwrite full implementation. This was seen in the OPTICOM and solid waste shredding cases. Thus, federal officials ought to investigate when they can strategically utilize limited funds and eliminate the necessity of underwriting full implementation.

2. Large-scale innovations do not necessarily require federal aid. Resource recovery and the firefighting innovations are cases in point. The key to determining when federal aid is appropriate is understanding the element of risk in local government ecology.[58] Local officials risk little in committing local funds when the delivery of vital public services is threatened, as in a solid waste disposal crisis. The problem for federal officials is that what constitutes an interruption of vital public service, like the definition of "obscenity," depends on community standards. Thus, federal officials must trouble

themselves to investigate the local ecology of public administration to determine if massive aid is appropriate and needed.

3. To reiterate, federal officials need to pay more attention to
the problems that plague innovation during implementation
and incorporation. In granting capital and operating funds to
local governments, federal officials ought to ask themselves
what the likelihood is that local agencies will have the capacity
to carry on when federal aid inevitably ends. This question was
not properly addressed in the solid waste shredding, Project
Unique, and dial-a-bus cases; retrenchment or dampening of
the innovation, in varying degrees, was the result. In contrast,
federal officials at LEAA strategically used grants to the
Syracuse and Rochester police departments for training
purposes in the SRIP and Coordinated Team Patrol cases. The
grants were given after the innovation was underway and
became major factors in building local capacity for full
incorporation.

Technical Support

Technical support is an alternative to funding strategies
open to federal officials. It has been touted as an effective way to
supplement the local capacity to innovate. Unfortunately, the
experience with this type of intervention strategy in Syracuse
and Rochester shows that it should be used with extreme
caution. Federal consultants did more to harm the Campus
Plan than to help it. They assisted local officials in designing a
program that simply did not address local needs. Much the
same was true in the Rochester dial-a-bus case. On the other
hand, outside consultation was gratefully accepted in UFIRS,
but only after the innovation had been adopted. Thus, federal
technical assistance is probably more appropriate during
implementation and incorporation. If it is given prior to
adoption, it should be geared to local wishes, rather than
attempt to form local attitudes.

Lobbying

Finally, lobbying by federal officials for local innovation
may occasionally be helpful. For example, the testimony of
federal officials in Rochester helped to convince the county

legislature to approve resource recovery. In the proper context, well timed and placed expert federal testimony can be an effective strategy for inducing local change. In an era of increasing technological complexity, local legislators sometimes desire the assurance of outside experts that they are taking the proper course of action. However, federal activity of this sort can be resented at the local level, unless such assistance has been requested by local decision makers. This is a strategy to be used with great discretion.

Notes

1. See Donald E. Cunningham, John R. Craig, and Theodore W. Schlie, eds., *Technological Innovation: The Experimental R&D Incentives Program* (Boulder, Colo.: Westview Press, 1977).

2. William Baumol, "Macroeconomics of Unbalanced Growth: The Anatomy of Urban Crisis," *American Economic Review* 57, no. 3 (June 1967):415-26. For a critical review of the literature on the "innovativeness" of public organizations, see J. David Roessner, "Incentives to Innovate in Public and Private Organizations," *Administration and Society* 9, no. 3 (November 1977):341-65.

3. Alan L. Frohman, "Fighting Fires: Only the Truck Is New," *Technology Review* 75, no. 6 (May 1973):36.

4. See Richard Nelson, *The Moon and the Ghetto* (New York: W. W. Norton, 1977); and W. Henry Lambright, *Governing Science and Technology* (New York: Oxford University Press, 1976), chapter 4.

5. George Downs and Lawrence B. Mohr, "Conceptual Issues in the Study of Innovation," *Administrative Science Quarterly* 21:700-14.

6. E. M. Rogers and F. Floyd Shoemaker, *Communication of Innovations* (New York: The Free Press, 1971).

7. Everett M. Rogers, J. D. Eveland, and Constance Klepper, *The Innovation Process in Public Organizations*, a report to the National Science Foundation by the University of Michigan, March 1977, chapter 1.

8. Robert L. Crain et al., *The Politics of Community Conflict: The Fluoridation Decision* (New York: Bobbs-Merrill Co. 1969).

9. See, for example, Elinor Ostrom, ed., *The Delivery of Urban Services* (Beverly Hills, Calif.: Sage Publications, 1976); and Robert L. Lineberry, *Equality and Urban Policy* (Beverly Hills, Calif.: Sage Publications, 1977).

10. Robert A. Dahl, *Who Governs?* (New Haven, Conn.: Yale University Press, 1962).

11. For a critical review of the community power literature, see David M. Ricci, *Community Power and Democratic Theory* (New York: Random House, 1971); and Eugene Lewis, *The Urban Political System* (Hinsdale, Ill.: The Dryden Press, 1973).

12. Wallace S. Sayre and Herbert Kaufman, *Governing New York City* (New York: Russell Sage Foundation, 1960).

13. This is similar to the model used by Rogers et al. in *The Innovation Process in Public Organizations*.

14. Ibid.

15. See, for example, Jeffrey L. Pressman and Aaron B. Wildavsky, *Implementation* (Berkeley, Calif.: University of California Press, 1973); and Eugene Bardach, *The Implementation Game* (Cambridge, Mass.: MIT Press, 1977).

16. Robert Yin et al., *Changing Urban Bureaucracies: How New Practices Become Routinized.* Report prepared under a grant from the National Science Foundation, R-2277-NSF, March 1978.

17. See Langdon Winner, *Autonomous Technology: Technics Out-of-Control as a Theme in Political Thought* (Cambridge, Mass.: MIT Press, 1977).

18. Downs and Mohr, "Conceptual Issues."

19. Our use of the concept "minimum winning coalition" is not derived from the "game theory" perspective of the literature on legislative coalitions. Rather, our use is more in line with the perspective of organization theory. See, for example, James D. Thompson, *Organizations in Action* (New York: McGraw-Hill, 1967).

20. Roscoe C. Martin, Frank J. Munger, et al., *Decisions in Syracuse*, Anchor Edition (Garden City, N.Y.: Doubleday, 1961).

21. Some of this difference is accounted for by the fact that Rochester includes water and street lighting under public works and Syracuse does not. However, it should be pointed out that Rochester also spends disproportionately more for water and street lighting than Syracuse.

22. Martin, et al., *Decisions in Syracuse.*

23. This section is drawn from Blake McKelvey, *Rochester on the Genesee* (Syracuse, N.Y.: Syracuse University Press, 1973); and Monroe County, *Preface to Tomorrow*, 1976.

24. League of Women Voters of the Syracuse Metropolitan Area, *Patterns of Government in Onondaga County* (Syracuse, N.Y., 1970), 12.

25. Many of the facts in this section are from Blake McKelvey, "The

Last Eleven Mayors, the First Eleven Managers, and Twenty County Chairmen," *Rochester History* 32, no. 2 (April 1970).

26. Center for Governmental Research Inc., *The Governance of Rochester*, a staff report to the Rochester Charter Commission, May 1973.

27. The mayor is a member of the council and is elected by a majority vote of the council. Five members of the council are elected at large, and four represent districts.

28. Center for Governmental Research, Inc., *Governance of Rochester*, p. 39.

29. Ibid, p. 10.

30. For varying views of technology and a discussion of technology as "tools," see Emmanuel G. Mesthene, *Technological Change* (New York: New American Library, 1970).

31. For a broad discussion of the concept of "performance gap," see Anthony Downs, *Inside Bureaucracy* (Boston: Little, Brown, and Company, 1967), chapters 14-16; for an application of the concept of "performance gap" to municipal decisions regarding innovation, see Irwin Feller et al., *Diffusion of Innovations in Municipal Governments*, a report to the National Science Foundation by the Pennsylvania State University, June 1976, chapter 4.

32. Stephen Zwerling, *Mass Transit and the Politics of Technology: A Study of BART and the San Francisco Bay Area* (New York: Praeger, 1974).

33. Downs, *Inside Bureaucracy*.

34. For a useful and brief discussion of the literature on organizational decision making, see Victor A. Thompson, *Decision Theory, Pure and Applied* (New York: General Learning Press, 1971).

35. Rogers et al., *Innovation Process*.

36. SCAN is a pseudonym for Silent Communication Alarm Network. This system, designed by NASA's Jet Propulsion Laboratory, is capable of pinpointing the source of an alarm and was designed to deal with the problem of school violence. See W. Henry Lambright and Albert H. Teich, principal investigators, *Federal Laboratories and Technology Transfer: Institutions, Linkages, and Processes*, a report on a study for the National Science Foundation (Syracuse and Binghamton, N.Y.: Syracuse University Research Corporation and the State University of New York at Binghamton, 1974). 12.

37. See Francis E. Rourke, "Variations in Agency Power," in Francis E. Rourke, ed., *Bureaucratic Power in National Politics* (Boston: Little Brown, and Company, 1965), 240-62.

38. The strategies used in "selling" a technological innovation in

the city are similar to those used at the national level. See Lambright, *Governing Science and Technology.*

39. For a detailed discussion of federal demonstrations, see W. S. Baer et al., *Analysis of Federally Funded Demonstration Projects,* The Rand Corporation, R-1926-DOC, April 1976.

40. There is a great deal of literature on citizen participation in urban settings which suggests this is the case. See, for example, Sherry R. Arnstein, "A Ladder of Citizen Participation in the U.S.A.," *Town Planning Institute Journal 51* (April 1971):176-82; and Earl M. Blecher, *Advocacy Planning for Urban Development* (New York: Praeger, 1971).

41. For a lucid but less optimistic view of the role of citizens in bureaucratic decision making, see Eugene Lewis, *American Politics in a Bureaucratic Age: Citizens, Constituents, Clients, and Victims* (Cambridge, Mass.: Winthrop Publishers, Inc., 1977).

42. The broker function in technological innovation is discussed at greater length in W. Henry Lambright and Albert H. Teich, "Technology Transfer as a Problem in Interorganizational Relationships," *Administration and Society* 8, no. 1 (May 1976):29-53.

43. Compare Herbert Kaufman, "Why Change is Dampened," chapter 3 in *The Limits of Organizational Change* (University, Alabama: The University of Alabama Press, 1971). While Kaufman speaks in terms of "dampening" as something to be overcome if organizational death is to be avoided, we argue that dampening can also be a conscious strategy to stay alive.

44. Kenneth L. Kraemer, for example, has discussed the cost pitfalls in computer technology transfer. See Kenneth L. Kraemer, "Local Government, Information Systems and Technology Transfer: Evaluating Some Common Assertions About Computer Application Transfer," *Public Administration Review* 4, (July/August 1977):368-82.

45. What Anthony Downs says of zealots and getting *agencies* underway applies also to innovations. See Downs, *Inside Bureaucracy.*

46. The most extensive work on the incorporation phase of the innovation process is that by Yin et al., *Changing Urban Bureaucracies.*

47. This is documented in the full case study, "Innovations in the Syracuse Police Department: Two Case Studies," in the Case Studies of Innovation in Syracuse, New York, volume of the final report of this study.

48. We chose not to discuss these attributes in chapter 4 since they are even less an inherent characteristic of a technology than are other

attributes. Cost and service efficiency can be measured only after application of the technology.

49. Rourke, *Bureaucratic Power.*

50. Rogers et al., *Innovation Process.*

51. See Downs, *Inside Bureaucracy,* for a detailed description of types of bureaucratic personalities.

52. This concept is borrowed from Jeffrey L. Pressman, *Federal Programs and City Politics* (Berkeley, Calif.: University of California Press, 1975), chapter 2, "The Receptacle: Oakland's Political System."

53. This is also a major recommendation of the report by Yin et al., *Changing Urban Bureaucracies.*

54. For a more detailed discussion of the role of state government in local innovation, see Paul J. Flynn, James D. Carroll, and Thomas A. Dorsey, "Vertical Coalitions for Technology Transfer: Toward an Understanding of Intergovernmental Technology," a paper delivered at the Annual Meeting of the American Political Science Association, Washington, D.C., September, 1977.

55. Yin argues that great discrimination is needed by federal officials before proceeding with any intervention in local innovation processes. External change agents must be sensitive to the needs of different localities. See Yin et al., *Changing Urban Bureaucracies.*

56. For a discussion of mayoral attitudes toward innovation, see Arnold M. Howitt, "Mayors and Policy Innovation," a paper prepared for the Annual Meeting of the American Political Science Association, Washington, D.C., September 1977.

57. See Flynn et al., "Vertical Coalitions," for a full discussion of patterns of federal involvement in the Syracuse–Rochester cases.

58. The concept of ecology in public administration is from John Gaus, *Reflections on Public Administration* (University, Ala.: University of Alabama Press, 1947), 6-19.

Index